KINETIC TRANSFORMATION

By:

M. Nathaniel Gampel

Copyright

Kinetic Transformation

By: M. Nathaniel Gampel

Published by:

Simpel and Associates, LLC
136 Lexington Ave.
Edison, NJ 08816

www.simpelandassociates.com

For permissions contact:
Nathan Gampel
info@simpelandassociates.com

Cover by: Rebecca Irene Lopez, www.bettacreates.com

ISBN: 978-0-578-81680-7

Dedication

To my best friend, my confidant and my lifelong partner in crime, my wife Sara. None of this and I mean none of it would be possible without you. Living with me for more than 20 years, you have met my unending snowstorms in July and heatwaves in January with a smile and support. I can never thank you enough for all you do every day and I love you dearly.

To my children, Rebecca, Isaac, and David. You guys are just awesome. Thanks for being so flexible with me as I found my voice and way in life. Thank you for teaching me and always giving me the courage to find my way back.

To my father, the original force of nature, Dr. Ezra Gampel. Thank you for teaching me the value of hard work and how to never give up. Thank you for being there when I needed you most and for always being a true believer.

Disclaimer

This is a work of fiction. Names, characters, businesses, places, events, locales, and incidents are either the products of the author's imagination or used in a fictitious manner. Any resemblance to actual persons, living or dead, or actual events is purely coincidental.

Table of Contents

Introduction

I can't believe it has been four years since the night it all changed.

Four years ago, my family and I were on the first vacation we'd taken in two years. It was one of my famous adventure trips where the entire family agreed to spend our days seeing a major city – on foot.

This time, we picked my third favorite place in the world, San Francisco. I had been planning this trip for months and spoke about it to just about anyone who would listen. Of course, like everything else in my life up to that point, it was ruined before I even got on the plane.

The day before we hit the road, I came to the realization that after years of working to get into one of the best consultancies in the world, my career there was coming to an end. It was simply not working out and like so many jobs before, it was time to move on.

Second verse, same as the first – only this time, something was different. I just couldn't do it anymore. For so many years I busted my hump. I had worked a full-time day job and gone to school at night. I was a responsible husband and parent, but no matter how hard I tried, I could not find happiness in my career. I was in my late thirties and lost. Worst of all, I was adrift while in the company of the people I loved most.

In the middle of yet another late-night walk of brooding solitude, something snapped. The walls of my self-confidence melted. Despite my degrees, resume, and accomplishments, I *knew* my career was over.

And I knew I was no good.

After about three hours of walking, it was just after midnight and I headed back to the room where my family slept. Dejected and with nowhere else to go, I did something I hadn't done for a while – I decided to watch some music videos.

As I searched for something to watch the irony hit me. When I was a child, even though I was an avid music fan, I did not have music television to satisfy my desire to see the latest music videos. And yet as an adult, with every music video I could ever want available online, it had been years since I indulged what had once been a consuming passion.

In that moment I realized I had lost the sense of who I was. I had misplaced the boy who dreamed of greatness and morphed into someone who'd allowed the corporate world and his own feelings of dissatisfaction to suppress everything – even the fun stuff.

Determined to shake things up, I remembered a few weeks earlier hearing a song called "Wake Me Up" by an artist who would become one of my favorites, Avicii. Although I felt like I might be a little old for this genre of music, I really liked the rhythm and figured it was worth a shot.

What started with one video turned into a two hour binge watching session. As my eyelids began to sag, I decided to watch one more video for a song I had not heard before called *Broken Arrows*.[1]

Have you ever watched the high jump? I have always been fascinated by the event. Athletes somehow defy gravity and hurl themselves over a horizontal bar suspended between two poles. I am mesmerized by the technique. Logic tells you the athletes should dive over the bar or try to straddle it. Instead, they go over *with their backs facing the ground.* The technique is named "The Fosbury Flop" for the guy who tried it first, Dick Fosbury.

Earlier in his career Mr. Fosbury had struggled to gain enough height with the traditional "scissors method" and decided to work on something completely different. Because of increased leverage (or voodoo), Fosbury determined to go over the bar "bass ackwards" and eventually won the Gold Medal at the 1968 Olympic Games in Mexico City.

Well, leave it to Avicii to spin a tale about a Dick Fosbury-esque character finding the inspiration for this novel approach from his daughter.[2]

The video begins with a down and out high jumper. A single

dad and big-time loser, who can't get the local barmaid to dance even though he is insanely handsome and in great shape. All his daughter wants is her father's attention and recognition for her budding mastery of gymnastics.

Things are not going well.

One day, the jumper suffers a crushing defeat of an undisclosed nature. When he arrives home full of anger and sadness, he notices his daughter too is affected by his failure. Only this time, instead of ignoring her and heading out to the bar, our high jumper decides to do something different. To take his daughter's mind off her troubles, he decides to teach her how to high jump.

After numerous attempts the girl is unable to make it over the bar. But then, inspiration strikes. After failing multiple times, the plucky young thing decides to employ her own gymnastics skills. Instead of charging the bar, she launches into a back handspring and clears the hurdle.

In a flash, the father realizes he has just received divine inspiration.

The music swells as the father applies his daughter's technique to his own jumping. With renewed confidence, the jumper goes on to victory and fame and, most importantly, salvation.

For whatever reason – fatigue, depression, one of those moments of clarity that visits in the night – the video speared my spirit. It spoke to me on levels you cannot imagine. I did a quick Google search and found our hero, Dick Fosbury, inventor of the Fosbury Flop.

As my sadness broke and I sat back in my chair, I looked over at my sleeping family. Not ten feet away was my daughter. Two years from graduating, she too was experiencing her own challenges. Like any teenage girl, she was going through her own transformation to adulthood in the confusing time known as high school.

An incredible singer, my daughter was a very artistic child in a prep school atmosphere. No matter the pressure to fit in, she never wavered in being true to herself and in the end, always ended up on top. From dance and singing competitions to leading her hockey team to the championships, her spirit to win and fearless confidence in herself made her a leader.

All this time, I'd been leaping headfirst into a career and crashing into the bar. If I did not change my approach, I would end up like the dad at the beginning of the video – broken and disillusioned.

Moments of clarity come along rarely – a handful of times in a lifespan. I recognized my chance and sitting in a dark hotel room, I vowed to change – to capture success and contentment once and for all. It dawned on me that perhaps my career was not working because instead of emulating my daughter and pursuing my passion, I had been chasing someone else's view for who I should be. Maybe I was afraid to be myself?

I opened my computer and spent the next hour thinking about who I was and what I really loved to do.

I kept returning to the happiest time in my professional life, graduate school.

It was in grad school that I discovered the profession of change management. I thought about papers I'd written – my fledgling theories on how change worked and how it could be managed better.

With a second wind, I began to write what would become a business plan for a new company. A company built on a philosophy started in graduate school and refined over a twenty-plus year career leading massive change programs for some of the leading companies in the world.

As page after page came to life, that old feeling of self-doubt fought its way to the front. Perhaps I was being too hasty. After all, it took me more than two decades to work my way into the leading consulting firms. Perhaps giving it all up to run on a dream was a little crazy.

I looked across the room again at my slumbering family. Every few years, I ended up in the same place – leaving a job I'd thought would be "the one." The unknown is always frightening. But I'd been sprinting on a professional hamster wheel for too long. I needed to dive headfirst (backwards) into my destiny or my cycle of frustration would keep repeating.

With a smile and a new favorite song on my lips, I put the final touches on my plan. I clicked "save," closed my laptop, thanked the heavens for my inspiration, and then slept as soundly as I ever had in my life. When the morning broke, I awoke with a smile. I knew something special had happened and I was ready to see it through.

A few weeks later my time with the consulting firm ended and I was on my own. Even with my new found confidence, the gusto from my late-night session in San Francisco was no match for the tsunami of fear that approached the closer we came to the mortgage payment.

I voiced my concerns to my wife. Only instead of telling me to "Take a job if you are worried," she said, "Go with your gut. See your idea through."

With Sara's confidence in hand, I hunkered down and pressed ahead.

Days went by with no calls. No interviews. No meetings. With the end of the next month and another round of bills edging closer I was ready to throw in the towel.

Then, the Universe intervened.

Out of the hundreds of resumes and proposals I had sent out, one struck paydirt. A small consulting firm needed an extra set of hands on a major change it was leading.

As the interview of my life concluded, I finished my spiel with a simple question, "What is the name of your company?"

The response...

"Fosbury Incorporated."

It was in that moment, I felt safe. I knew something greater was at work. At long last I was on track.

I was transformed.

And I have never looked back.

How to Use This Book

Every year, companies and the collective population spend billions in an attempt to manage change. From high priced consultants to the latest self-help book, we are all looking for an approach or a method to help us cut through the noise, devise a plan, and come out better on the other end.

My job as an organization psychologist and business transformation specialist puts me in the middle of change efforts at some of the largest and most meaningful companies in the world. In fact, helping these organizations successfully work through massive change is not only my job – it's my obsession.

I am the guy your company hires to show up and take command of a crazy merger or Private Equity-led carve out. Yeah, you know me – the mysterious leadership figure from nowhere charged with the responsibility of guiding hundreds or even thousands of people from Strategic Point A to Strategic Point Z in as seamless a fashion as possible.

I am the guy you first hear about in a senior leadership meeting and talk about at the water cooler. I am also the guy you have to live with day in and out for six months (or longer), then I disappear like Kaiser Soze.[3]

If I did my job right, the big problem was solved, and you feel confident and empowered. What's more, you and I are probably friends to this day, and you are reading my book because you saw my name and wanted to support me (thanks). Happens all the time – even in my line of work – and it is my relationships with people that keep me going when the skies turn black and the water gets choppy.

On the flip side, if the process sucked, every time you see my name, you spit on the grass and it turns brown. You probably think you had everything under control before I came on site. Maybe you didn't get through the change at all or worse, don't think you did. Either way, you probably hate me.

Yes, evoking extreme, visceral reactions in the business

community is the life I selected. A funny choice for a self-conscious, shy, well-intentioned guy. But after 20+ years working at it I can honestly say I have finally mastered my trade.

But becoming the "guy they call" for change and transformation did not come easily. It took two master's degrees, decades of practice and of course, a ton of lumps. My route was hard, and I had a few fender benders along the way. But I am now happy and content.

When people who knew me years ago meet me today, they often can't do the math. How did I go from unhappy every few year job hopper to an emerging leader in anything?

The answer: through the experiences in my life and career, I have created a personal approach for leading through substantial times of change – something I call **The Simpel Kinetic Transformation Philosophy**©.[4]

Through The Simpel Kinetic Transformation Philosophy, I deliver results in record time by leading Transformational Initiatives for large clients (Fortune 500s), rising stars (companies with < $100MM in annual revenue) and everything in between.

In addition to my corporate work, I also use The Simpel Kinetic Transformation Philosophy in other areas of my practice with dramatic results. This includes helping other aspiring professionals and sernior leaders reach their career goals through my career coaching and public speaking businesses and my pro bono work helping those in need find work.

Probably because the path has been rocky, I feel driven to give back and help others who might learn from my experience. While this desire represents a cornerstone of my private practice and life's mission, I have always struggled with how to teach what I do.

Then, I had an epiphany.

Thinking back to the three months after the San Francisco trip, I realized it was during that time that I experienced the most intense and productive transformation of my life. As I lived through the change, my ideas crystalized, my daily life improved and I started blowing it up with major client after major client. I continue my upward trajectory today.

So, what changed? Why was this period different?

Unlike previous times of challenge, instead of just jumping to old habits, I consciously worked through my situation in a more fluid way. I replaced the rigid structure of "create a resume, apply, network, rinse and repeat" with a more flexible, open-minded approach that used experiences from my personal and professional lives to guide my actions. I didn't allow the process to manage me but rather used the time to experiment, gather data and refine my approach until it worked. This made the change very personal because I worked with **my change** using who **I was** and what **I knew** to meet the specific challenges as they came.

Because change is ever evolving and transformation is so impactful, you can only be successful when you approach it in this more personal way. Without this more introspective lens you are merely learning a generic system or producing generic data that may deliver a product but not a transformative outcome.

Without such an understanding, you are Jesse from *Breaking Bad*.[5] Sure, you might get the job done by following a recipe, but the results will be uneven because you do not understand "the chemistry" and you cannot replicate success with consistency. You copy a pattern, but you can't adapt and take a product, company, or person to the next level.

That's why Kinetic Transformation is a philosophy as opposed to a methodology. Sure, structure is needed to execute, especially when the project is large but that is secondary to approach. Once you learn how to understand yourself or your organization, what change is and how it works the rest will fall into place. Guaranteed.

To this end, my book presents The Simpel Kinetic Transformation Philosophy within the context of how it was created: through the transformational events of my life. By telling the story of how this philosophy appeared to me through my experiences, I hope you will see the pattern in your own life and understand how you can use your own tools and life lessons to win at change. Whether you are a CEO, an up-and-coming manager, or are simply looking to improve your life, I hope my story will help you better understand yourself and how **you have what it takes** to reach your own vision of success.

Section 1: Environment

It's funny, even after all these years, my wife and I still can't believe that we are adults. Only yesterday, we were children discovering ourselves and wondering what we wanted to be in life.

Time sure does fly.

Once upon a time I was a scared kid growing up in what felt like the wrong environment. My feelings manifested as a lack of focus during my high school days after which I started to grind toward succeeding in college and life. This pattern continued in an endless loop until the epiphany I spoke of in the introduction.

Corporate culture operates in a similar fashion. Whether an organization is a start-up, a carve out, or an established player with 50 years under its belt, how a company works today (also known as its culture) is an amalgamation of what it has done to date. The more you act in a certain way, the more inertia sets in and the harder it is to be flexible in the face of change.

This lack of flexibility is at the core of why many organizations fail when it comes to working through massive change events. Organizations, like people, become set in their ways; the weight of history makes change difficult to accept. The best organizations (and people) accept this reality and never stop forcing themselves to evolve and grow.

Getting to this ideal state of mastering change does not happen overnight. It begins with understanding change and how powerful properly managing it can be.

Change, like gravity and nuclear energy, represents an impactful and relentless force. Without it, life has no risk and ultimately no purpose. Change drives the world. Whether we like it or not, change gallops forward – right at us – on personal, professional, and global levels. We can either embrace change and learn to dance with it or we can be crushed under its relentless weight. The choice is ours.

Yet even in the face of this fact, I am often astounded by how poorly change management is practiced in the business world. I have worked on many $100 million projects where "change management" boiled down to an expense or the soft stuff that you just have to do to make the boss happy. With limited budgets, leaders naturally focus their time and money on "hard skills." Change management becomes relegated to the nice-looking presentations or analyses that tell you what you already know and seldom can do anything with. Change management becomes that work stream that eats up time, always butting in when you could be focused on something more important. And yet, in my experience, it is the ability to properly manage change that often drives whether a program is a failure or success.

This mistake is not limited to big business. We also underutilize the power of good change management on a personal level.

Think about going on a diet. You know there is a huge difference between a quick result fad diet and a sustainable one. The fad does not alter thinking – it seldom focuses on the underlying problems causing obesity. The fad addresses an immediate, Pavlovian need to make us feel we can have what we want when we want it.

A proper diet teaches how to adopt new eating habits often by changing how we view food. Long-term, change-centric diets have a far higher likelihood of success for obvious reasons. Still, nothing stopped me from recently spending $400 on a horrible program with terrible food and a commandment to limit my daily calorie intake to an unsustainable 1,000 calories! The bright packets and varied "food options" sucker me every time.

We are all just prone to grasp at "what's hot" and we especially latch onto anything if it promises to make us look and/or feel better. We want results – instantaneous results.

If we took all the money we'd spent and the time we'd wasted and made a proper investment in *change*, well, our landscapes would look a lot different and we would ultimately be happier.

Recognizing the Power of Change is the start of the journey to successful change management and is why the best change agents are always at the ready. These leaders never stop looking for the stimuli or disruptions to what some may call stability and seamlessly weave this knowledge into their response. They proactively address the stimuli before they become a problem. The very best leaders can almost do this with a predictive sensitivity or what I call **Organization ESP.**

Developing Organization ESP is not easy. It only happens when you understand yourself or in the case of business, the people and how the culture plays out in day to day activities.

As a transformation leader, I am often faced with the need to deliver fast results while in the quicksand of learning years of history in a very short amount of time. I must develop my Organization ESP while also delivering complex outcomes as I lead an organization through what will likely be a defining transformational program.

How do I do it?

I begin by gathering basic data and creating broad hypotheses that are tested and refined throughout the program. While many practitioners struggle with where to begin, I have found that it is often the most obvious places where the best data lies. After all, if we are heavily shaped by our surroundings, then why not start with the most obvious, observable factors and then test and learn from there?

For example, within minutes of meeting me, anyone will figure out that the primary influences in my life are.

- My family – the most important thing in my life
- Religion and career (a tie)
- Entrepreneurship
- An innate fear of change

Companies operate the same way. Without much depth, if you step back from any situation, there are likely obvious influences from which you can start building a story and structuring your analysis. Many people get lost in the data in search of the root cause when in fact, it is often the big and obvious things staring at you in the face that are really driving you forward.

As we will see, when you start by addressing the big obvious stuff, even small changes can have a disproportionate impact.

Like a martial arts expert, once you find the right pressure point, a little push can turn the tide in a significant way. Identifying the primary influencers, prioritizing them, and knowing when to push them lies at the core of any successful transformation. It is not about the tool but knowing what to use when for maximum impact.

Masters of change management know how to use accumulated skills and experiences as tools for working with change vs. being burdened down it. Because they understand how change works, they do not get distracted by it. Instead, they use what they know about themselves (or their organizations) to identify assets that are deployed as the change demands.

Knowing what change demands and when begins with understanding how to work with change or as I call it the **Basics of Change**. These ideas lie at the heart of the Simpel Kinetic Transformation model and have helped me gain control over things that seemed omnipresent. The Transformational Basics include:
- Cause and effect
- Doing the Change Dance
- Fearless honesty
- Staying the Course
- Understanding it is always personal

Cause and Effect

While change is unpredictable it never begins in a vacuum. Sometimes the stimuli are unintended; other times the recipient seeks them out. Either way, without something prodding the object to change, it will never happen. Our ability to identify, understand, and prioritize these stimuli are key determinants for success.

Think of yourself like an object floating through space. If nothing gets in the way, you will go on forever without ever slowing down.[6] Our habits are the same. Without a stimulus, nothing changes, and we will continue doing the same things again and again.

This is great news. It means once you can isolate and understand the stimuli, you can also ignite the change when and where you need it. By introducing good stimuli one can create opportunity for positive things. (Unfortunately, the converse is also true.) What works in business also serves in the private arena.

When I decided I needed to change my relationship with family, I changed the stimuli around me to include better people and activities. I met my wife, someone compatible with my values, and we continue to thrive twenty plus years down the road.

Doing the Dance

Unfortunately, leaders of change programs often get lost in the sea of stimuli and get overwhelmed. Keeping a close eye on stimuli and reacting to them fluidly are key tools in a successful Transformation Program Lead. It is not enough to have the tools, the person at the head of the change also needs to know when and how to use what's in the toolbox to deliver the desired results. (Anyone can own a hammer, a screwdriver, or a saw – not everyone can build a fine piece of furniture.) Doing the Dance is the difference between a rigid change effort (approaching a change situation with a rigid methodology) vs. one that bends and flexes with the rhythm of the change.

I have seen many transformational leaders who step on a lot of feet and cause a lot of misery. I've done it too. Sometimes, we insist on "leading the Tango" by introducing a never-ending stream of program management ideas and meet-

19

ings the result of which are bloated bureaucracy and frustration without any discernable improvement. Knowing how and when to use tools the right way is the true mark of a master change manager and it was true of me as well.

Fearless Honesty

You will not follow someone you do not trust. Change brings on emotional reactions – sometimes positive (happiness, thankfulness), sometimes negative (sadness, anger, or fear). A leader of a change needs to recognize the impact a change has on those involved and build trust among those affected. You can have all the technical knowledge in the world. If the people think you are shifty or "in it for yourself," your efforts will circle the drain.

The same holds true with your family, your friends, and your spouse.

Trust empowers a leader to do some amazing things.

Take one of the most sensitive types of projects that I do: outsourcing. I once did a survey during an outsourcing program. Guess what? The results showed the audience was afraid. Not surprising, but I still needed to drive fast action from the very people who would be impacted by the change. Interestingly, the survey also showed that the audience trusted management and felt that messaging from the top was sufficient. Using this knowledge, I steered everyone through the program, sometimes pushing them harder than conventional wisdom would suggest.

I reasoned the fear stemmed from uncertainty. So, the faster we made things clear, the better. If people trust my messaging, they will trust me when I tell them to "hold their nose and take the medicine." Well – they did, and we completed an end-to-end transformation of a Fortune 500 financial services company (including digital transformation, infrastructure, outsourcing, and marketing modernization) in record time. The project impacts the face of this decades' old player to this very day.

Because of this trust, over the course of the program my team knew that when I asked for things, I needed them – I was not on a power trip – I was not testing them. When the tempo picked up and we needed to hustle, they responded accordingly. Without trust, we would have tripped, fallen, and probably broken a whole lot of things.

The best part? I am still friends with almost everyone with whom I worked.

So, how do you build trust? It only comes through having the courage to be fearlessly honest. I will not lie and tell you it is easy. Looking someone in the eye and saying, "We are going to do this and that, then you will be out of a job" never brings me joy. But when I learned to "damn the torpedoes"[7] and practice absolute transparency, I found a valuable key to building strong and lasting relationships.

Staying the Course

Persistence and repetition, also called **Transformational Consistency**, are what I refer to as "the brakes for change." Many of us are familiar with the Kurt Lewin Change Management Model: "unfreeze, change, refreeze."[8] In a very over simplified nutshell the model suggests that for change to occur people need to be ready, they need to change, and then they need to do work to make the change stick. While this model forms the cornerstone of any change leader worth his (or her) salt, I would like to offer my own theory of how transformation works today.

Change is a constant. "Refreeze" is really more akin to crossing an event horizon.[9] Depending on the observer's perspective, we are either flying clear or caught in a gravitational force from which there is no escape (and on the other side of which may lurk disaster). Either way, change can come at any time to knock us free. We are constantly changing and never frozen. Being re-frozen, therefore, is a matter of perspective and how quickly we adjust depends on the practice we have (whether in athletics, business, or more personal matters).[10]

Persistence, particularly through repetition, is the best shield against the unpredictability of change. Practice creates forces like inertia that keep us on track. Even when our shields fail, our "muscle memory" helps us get back to or find "normal" faster (even when "normal" has been altered). The trick is to know when to apply the brakes vs. letting the momentum carry us along (e.g. what behavior we need to repeat vs. those we absolutely do not).

Transformational Consistency also affects our surroundings, which can be a good thing. Think about it. When you see someone dedicated to something, you get curious – you may even want to try it. That's why good leaders always set the right example

Understanding it is Always Personal

As you can probably tell by now, understanding relationships represents a key element of my philosophy, especially on an interpersonal level. The deeper you can understand relationships and how they impact you, the better your chances for achieving success in a change program.

Consider the powerful role relationships play when managing a large team. As we will see later, even if you have the best skills, if you cannot build personal relationships, you will flop like a collapsing souffle. Reflecting this, I always add a more "personal" element to my change programs from how I dress to the words and phrases that I use. The more time I spend relating to, empathizing with and understanding the people, the better the program's results.

If you are thinking these ideas seem like common sense, that is the point. Great leaders keep rules of engagement simple. They prefer to save energy for the work to be done rather than the process to be followed.

By looking for the big, obvious stuff about yourself or your organization, you have what you need to start identifying your assets and readying yourself for change. When coupled with simple rules for understanding change and how to work with it, you are ready to start on your path to Kinetic Transformation.

Key Takeaways:

- Leading through change is about understanding yourself, what change is and how to work with it
- Change, like gravity and nuclear energy, represents a never ending, impactful force of nature. Because you can't stop it, you must learn to live with it
- Masters of change never stop forcing themselves to evolve and grow. They look for and pro actively address stimuli before they become a problem
- The basics of change:
    - o Cause and effect – change is a result of stimuli we can observe and influence
    - o Doing the Change Dance – success is about learning to work with change
    - o Fearless honesty – always strive for honesty, no matter how painful
    - o Staying the Course – know when to reinforce and when to let go
    - o It is always personal – people need people especially when things are in flux

CHAPTER 1: I'M NOT AN IDIOT; I AM AN ARTIST

Imagine: the '80s – a traditional, religious home in New Jersey. Like every night, we're sitting at the dinner table. Dad grumbles about his day. Mom talks about all the latest news from the neighborhood. We go around the table and share. Then, my annoying sister, the only one who knows my deepest secret, decides to get even with me for something I do not even remember.

"So, Nathan, tell Mom and Dad what you want to be when you grow up."

Silence settles over the table like an inversion layer of smog. My mother leans forward, eyes sparkling with the tears she intends to shed the moment she hears the words she's awaited since the moment of my birth: *I want to be a doctor.*

Four sets of eyes bore into me. I shift in my seat, suddenly ravenous for the matzo ball soup, which, only moments ago, I was pretty sure they force fed to prisoners in Russian gulags. I spoon away until my father's voice echoes like distant thunder.

"Nathan."

With the casual nonchalance of a pickpocket caught in the act, I shrug. "An artist," I say. "I want to be an artist."

Four other spoons clack into bowls. Dad shakes his head and makes a sputtering sound. Mom rolls her eyes. "Stop with the bullshit. One of these days, would it kill you to take something seriously?"

Did it happen exactly that way? Maybe...maybe not. But, during my adolescent years, before parents at least made a pretense of sensitivity towards their children's "feelings," I am sure they would have rather heard the words "mob accountant" than "artist."

My culture prizes excellence and giving back to society. The overwhelming majority of people in my circle would never contemplate such an impractical profession. Our balancing act between the two worlds – physical and metaphysical – leans heavily towards pragmatism. A disproportionate number of my friends and associates eased into traditional slots in medicine, law, and banking. A few of the risk takers went into "computers."

Back in the day in my hyper driven community, even the thought of calling oneself an artist would make a parent cringe. I can visualize my mother's face as she reads the word then bites her lips, slightly *verklempt.*

My self-doubt stemming from being an artist in an accountant's world debilitated me. This led me, on more than one occasion to tell my wife in no uncertain terms that our lives were over, and we would never amount to anything. My thinking poisoned my mind and hurt those around me.

But even after all this, here I sit, tapping away at the keys – putting together a book – and thrilled to wake up every day.

How did I transform my thinking?

If I denied my good fortune, I'd be a liar. I was lucky to be exposed to good people and life lessons destined to keep me on track and to give me the strength to keep on fighting. My wife stands at the head of the line. Without her strength and support. I would not have the stamina or the will to speak in complete sentences.

Thinking about this question more scientifically, I think what helped me find the light when so many others who were close to me did not was the recognition that no matter what, I:

- Had goals,
- Refused to accept my "fate,"
- Did my best and
- Never lied.

If nothing else, I've spent a good deal of my life searching for truth. Not as clear cut as it may sound. You see, even when I was "killing it" at work, my incongruence made me feel like an imposter. To disprove my life of public deception, I drove myself hard. I pushed myself to accomplish more...and more...and still more.

Of course, the grinding rat race cannot continue forever, especially for creative free spirits like me. We are just different. We don't fit into any of the boxes – and for me, this was especially true of the boxes my parents had already selected for me. You know how that goes.

"Son, you can be anything you want as long as it ends in '...ologist.'" You can be a ...Anesthesiologist...Dermatologist... Radiologist? Pick anyone you want."

Whenever I tried to shoehorn my size "different" life into the wingtips I was expected to fill, I felt like a liar and created increasing inner conflict. I chased one opportunity after the next with the same results – crash and burn.

Then, a few years ago, everything changed. During my second year at Simpel and Associates, our first slow period set in and Friedrich Nietzsche's infamous observation dropped on my life like a falling piano: "When you look long into an abyss, the abyss also looks into you."[11] As anyone with their own business knows all too well, the chasm of "no business" is terrifying.

As I struggled through a summer of hell, lost in a stifling sea of who am I and what do I want to be, I finally reached my breaking point. Then, my amazing wife changed my life. She asked, "Why are you trying to be the next Big 4 consulting firm? Just be yourself and you will do great."

As I contemplated her advice, my father, the great Dr. Gampel, in his classic old school parenting way, chimed in (although with a little less tact). "Nathan, stop being useless, just write, do something productive, and you will feel better."

I figured, *What the hell* – and I started to write.

I've never thought of myself as a good writer – I don't compose songs – so, I was a little lost about the, you know, where to start part. But rather than face another brow beating, I sat down at the ole laptop and started pounding away about my life and what I think about business.

As one page turned into ten, something happened; for the first time I felt right. I was not doing what "they" wanted me to do. For the first time, I was being artistic. I was writing, and it felt great!

More words spilled onto the screen, my slow period eventually ended, and we have enjoyed years of gangbuster growth. I was saved, "born again," or whatever you want to call it, and ready to take on my life as an adult – for real this time.

Time moved on and my book project took a back seat. I had to make money to support my family and, to be honest, I enjoyed assuming the mantle of a recognized leader in the space of my choosing.

After a few months, I finally found time to return to the writing. I read through what I had. I liked the general concept, but the book felt dishonest. The stories came across like generic, robotic studies – as artificial as every other training book I've ever read. While the tales represented work-related challenges my colleagues and I had faced, I felt like I was trivializing them – substituting "lessons" and "facts" for the emotional blood we'd spilled as we practiced Change Management. I believed the math (and I still do): most change programs fail, which means most methodologies fall short.

I knew I needed a different approach.

If I intended to explain my emotions, I had to understand myself and what it meant to confront the abyss. When I looked at the details of my life and career, I saw success – great experiences – financial rewards. But – isn't there always a "but" – I *felt* like a failure.

The apparent absurdity did not make sense – the paradox of situational depression.

Something needed to give. I decided to attack the dilemma as I did any other project – I began by defining my strategy. Who am I? What do I value? What do I really want?

The initial assessment proved inconclusive. Was I a marketer? A consultant? A general manager?

Then it hit me – and I "time traveled" in my head back to a dinner table, an annoying sister, and the stunned looks on my parents' faces. I knew.

I am an artist.

I am who I choose (or need) to be. I morph according to the whims and requirements of my clients. Within my chosen "life lane," I approximate De Niro, Brando, Bale, and Jolie (okay, I'm not good looking enough, but you get the point) – a method actor. I inhabit the role I am called to fulfil.

Once I opened my eyes – once I recognized my reality – I could accept what I had accomplished and knew where I wanted to go.

**

Transformational change, as demonstrated in these pages, is a multi-layered process with the added challenge of emotion distorting reality. When this level of change is upon us, it is easy to be quickly overwhelmed by the pressure and multitude of tasks at hand. But, when we understand who we are rather than the label we are given we begin to see things differently. We learn to view ourselves and our experiences as resources and as a source of strength. We can then leverage the power of transformation to exceed our expectations.

In our professional lives, we often experience these massive changes as "managed projects" or what I call **Transformational Initiatives**. Every organization either encounters or launches them in response to or in anticipation of massive change. The initiatives represent a fundamental determinant of a company's longevity and success. If a company cannot adapt, it will eventually die. (Ask anyone who used to produce butter churns – good luck!)

Like all things, Transformational Initiatives possess their own rhythm. The managers, consultants, colleagues, or team leaders overseeing an Initiative are called **Transformational Leads.** Their role is to oversee goal setting and alignment and to ensure that the Initiative reaches its objectives.

Let's bring this down to a more personal level.

What is the one transformational experience we all encounter? The death of a loved one. When Elisabeth Kubler Ross released *Death and Dying*[12] in 1977, her "five stages of grief" changed the way counselors, funeral directors, and pastors deal with the bereaved. Now, almost everyone knows about – or has endured – denial, anger, bargaining, depression, and acceptance. Knowing about them will neither stop the stages from appearing nor give us much comfort when they descend. Since we are unique, we may experience them in a different order, but their impact remains profound. When death comes – as it always does – while we might understand the process, the changes and emotions surrounding the event invariably cause us to act in ways outside our norm and to do things we would never consider under "normal" circumstances.

People in organizations similarly struggle during transformational programs. They know they are going to work hard and that there is going to be uncertainty but they don't know when those feelings may emerge. They know there will be fear but they don't know when it will come or what will set it off the most. This can lead to confusion and loss of momentum that can doom a change from the bottom up.

Masters of change understand these cycles and how large-scale change can affect us, our organizations and its people. They take the time to understand who the organization is and what it has to offer and use these resources to adapt their response as the change unfolds. These leaders are not afraid of change but rather are accustomed to finding answers as they work through the patterns of the program.

When you approach change in this way, with a bias to action as you work with change, you begin to view yourself in a position of power with the clarity of purpose and tools to get the job done. Instead of saying "I can't do it because..." you begin to think in terms of "I can start by doing such and such, see where it goes and then adjust or invest as the need demands."

This change of mindset is hard for many but when done properly can provide an empowering jolt to action that gets you moving with confidence and agility.

Large transformational change has the power to be very disruptive. It can redefine how people, families, and organizations operate. It is fraught with peril but also reward. After all, with high risk comes high return. When companies and individuals embrace this power and learn to work with it, there is no telling where they can end up.

Look at me. I began as one thing, and changed into something else. From an educated business professional locked into a life that did not fit, I transformed into what I always wanted to be; an artist. By recognizing who I really was and working through the change with the tools I possessed I found success and happiness in ways I never could have imagined and you can too.

Who am I? I am an *artist*!

Key Takeaways:

- To thine own self be true. No matter the chal lenge, success requires viewing yourself as some one with capabilities rather than a label
- Just doing something with purpose and focus is better than doing nothing and can lead to out comes you never imagined
- Transformational change is a multi-layered process with the potential for emotions to distort reality

- Change has power. If you understand how it works and learn to work with it, the process itself can unleash momentum (Kinetic Transform ation) and drive you forward to success

CHAPTER 2: LESSONS FROM A SHMATA

One morning I decided to do something naughty. It was 8:30 AM on a Tuesday and I decided to take an extra-long shower. It wasn't particularly cold outside, and I had a lot to do but I figured what the heck, I deserved it.

After a while, I realized it was time to get going. I soaked up as much warmth as I could, shut off the water, and stepped out in search of a towel. In my haze I noticed an old, raggedy- looking "thing" clinging to the bathtub like a faded red, white, and blue barnacle. Not wanting to cover my newly cleaned epidermis with what once might have been terrycloth, I kicked it onto the floor – an extension to the shower mat.

As I felt the gnarled cloth under my feet, I knew I'd made the right decision. No old towel for me – this was *my special time.*

The next morning, the towel was back – like the stray cat you made the mistake of feeding once. It (the towel, not the cat) had reacquired its perch on the tile surrounding the tub.

Then, just like that, nostalgia flowed through my mind like smoke.

We'd bought the towel, a gaudy *homage* to national pride, on a trip to the beach when our kids were little. We had four people back then (a mom, a dad, and two kids) and only two towels. In those days – both of us working and a low-end washer/dryer (one of those stackable things) – we more-than-occasionally ran short of linens. On one such occasion, we were on our way to the beach and stopped at a local pharmacy to purchase this now defunct artifact.

For whatever reason, looking at the forlorn and worn towel brought back memories of that day. I thought of my stunning wife – her blonde locks blowing in the ocean breeze, her bronze skin soaking up the summer sun. I remembered our beautiful Rebecca running and giggling as my wife tried to corral her. I thought about Isaac, sensitive and thoughtful even then, at first afraid of the ocean and then a little human dolphin.

The towel traveled with us when I took the children to a friend's summer home in Vermont. I recalled wrapping up my brave Isaac after he was the first person to jump off a 20-foot cliff into a raging river.

Then, I remembered someone unexpected – my grand-mother. Dina was a private school kindergarten teacher for approximately a hundred years. She had all the sugar and spice of Mary Poppins and made great homemade potato chips to boot.

In addition to her teaching, Dina was a devoted home-maker. An outstanding cook, she took meticulous care of her modest, Bronx-special, attached row home. When she wasn't cooking, she was cleaning: upstairs, downstairs, va-cuuming, bleaching, you name it.

Whenever I encountered grandma as she cleaned, a *shmata* (cleaning rag) was never far behind. God forbid we should ever throw away an outgrown or torn shirt. Once in grandma's hands, it was reborn as a new tool, a new *shmata.*

Back when times were simpler, people valued their possessions much more. Even the meekest item could be made into something useful if only grandma could get there before it went into the garbage.

Reflecting on my grandmother, I began to realize some things about myself. I am a person from a traditional home with traditional values where value is…well… valued. I often find disproportionate significance in small or mundane items because I cherish the thoughts or feelings that accompany them.

Sometimes it is good to value the simple things because they help you appreciate what you have and avoid being frivolous. At the same time, it is important to not take this too far because it can hold you back. Like when my value obsession has gotten in the way of me taking a risk that I should have taken to better myself and my business.

Yes, each of us has a history and a story to tell. Sometimes it can be hard to tell that story and that is where shmatas come in.

Shamatas are the visible, cultural artifacts in our lives and can represent important sources of data about who we are and where we come from. They are usually easy to find if we only know to look.

Indeed, shmatas are an important source of data that I often use in the earliest stages of a Transformation Initiative. Sound crazy? Read on…

Consultants hate the word "culture." We all know it's real and we all recognize its importance. But, if you ever try to sell a "culture project," you understand that rejection is not far away because while everyone instinctively knows what culture is, no one can adequately describe it or measure it to any degree of accuracy.

Culture is "How we do things around here" or "Our secret sauce." Corporate culture is what makes one global consultancy say they are different from another (so they can charge three times the going rate). Culture represents brand history and can prove overwhelming to distill into simple sentences.

Consultants are perpetual outsiders. I am often brought into situations that are tumultuous and I need to quickly fit in, grab the reins and start making a difference right away. This of course is no easy task but I have learned over the years how to use the environment to quickly gather the information I need to be successful.

Shmatas are the artifacts I often look for first because they are easy to find and the data they provide can often tell me more about employees and morale than days of analysis. The data gleaned from a shmata is often not found in a standard assessment tool and it comes in an easy to digest form that enables quick understanding and integration into any approach. Once I am armed with this data I can make relationships faster which in turn helps to make the change stick.

Case in point, I once led a transformation at a leading global digital media services group. This company began its life as a reseller of music and was now a global provider of digital products.

I was engaged to help the company shift into a high performing organization by introducing a new organization function called an Enterprise Project Management Office (EPMO). For those less familiar, an EPMO standardizes how work is delivered and reported. It includes processes to align strategy, identify associated work (projects) and oversee successful delivery of the work by the team. If this sounds complicated it should. Implementing changes of this nature to a 100-year old business is every bit as easy as stopping an Indy car by dragging your feet.

As I got to know the team, I quickly realized this project was going to be a lot harder than I initially imagined. Though in my eyes many of the processes I planned to implement seemed like common sense, this company had never even heard of many of the most basic terms I planned to use. The organization had never worked this way (and frankly never needed to) but now, market forces were driving it to change. Imagine teaching 1,000 people across the globe a new language while delivering daily for clients. It was that hard.

With more time on site with the client, I began to notice a theme. Wherever I looked I saw artifacts from the entertainment industry. From posters to guitars and gold discs, there was a cornucopia of awesome stuff forgotten in plain sight.

My curiosity drove me to ask questions. I learned this had once been a proud company that was simply stuck in what it was instead of what it needed to be. The company could no longer function as a traditional music reseller even though its culture and related artifacts seemed to scream otherwise. In fact, what was driving the transformation was more than a need for new and efficient ways of working. The entire mindset needed a massive overhaul.

Transformation leads like me see situations like this all the time. Sometimes the juice is not worth the squeeze and the company or people are simply too far gone to salvage. Other times where one may see failure and an aging workforce another set of eyes may see a diamond in the rough. The best transformation leads need to be able to quickly make this distinction and use this knowledge to pursue a course of action. A little cold hearted, I know, but this is how it works in our personal lives as well. In a world of limited resources, we make the best bets we can to deliver the highest likelihood of success.

This organization's shmatas indicated a lot of potential. Instead of an aging, out of touch workforce, I saw a history of fun people who grew up together. People who saw good times and bad times. People who developed a bond around music, the arts and most of all their clients. A dedicated, hardworking team... that I could work with.

To help the team change, I realized I would have to quickly develop connections. I made a mental note of every artifact I saw and found a way to weave this knowledge into every introductory conversation. Whether I was with the CEO or an administrative assistant, I worked in a funny comment or fact about the various artwork throughout the office. "Did you know Chuck Berry played a Gibson ED model like the one hanging in the Reception Area?"

At first people looked at me funny. Like "why are you commenting on our noise." But after only a few days something changed. The team began to find my purposeful recognition of the culture endearing. They began to see me as someone who "got it" – someone they talk to. They quit seeing me as "the outside consultant" and accepted me as a member of the team.

By taking the time to become aware of our surroundings, we can often find the easiest and most important drivers for success. Yes, the answer is often staring us right in the face if we only stop to look.

Since we are on the topic of the media company project, it is probably as good a time as any to talk about a term you will see throughout this book: "Agile."

When people first hear about The Simpel Kinetic Transformation Philosophy, they immediately think I am an Agile[13] coach or training master. In truth, techniques based on the Agile management approach are just a small percentage of the tools I use in my expansive medicine cabinet.

As I work through programs, I am constantly diagnosing and writing prescriptions for different approaches to solve problems as they arise. This ability to understand the program and the people it is impacting and to use this knowledge to drive a program forward in a more purposeful way are important and distinct skills possessed by leaders of big change initiatives.

While I certainly leverage what are known as "Agile concepts" in my work, I am not limited. Rather, I blend multiple tools and techniques from a variety of methodologies. The tool is not as important as knowing basic concepts and when to act. This is one of the core reasons my philosophy is so easy to adapt. You don't need years of schooling or mastery of hundreds of tools to get there. With the right basic principles and courage to test and act, you can accomplish anything and even create your own tools along the way.

Taking a flexible, personal approach to change even works when implementing Agile itself.

Anyone who has implemented Agile knows it is incredibly difficult and prone to failure. Especially when used outside of IT organizations.

As companies race to the fad of "becoming Agile" they often realize too late that Agile, a process aptly named to imply flexibility, can actually be a costly and potentially rigid process that does not play well with others. As a result, a great many organizations that have aspired to become Agile wind up with a confused and misfunctioning hybrid.

Contrast that with using Agile at the right time and in the right way. These organizations often find that Agile techniques provide the perfect tool to change behaviors fast, get a product to market very quick, or get something done now... now...now.

Key ingredients of the Agile approach are an overflow of repetition and ceremony, breaking work into manageable chunks and aligning accountability for quick decision making that removes barriers to progress. Making all this work together takes a lot of skill and can be very overwhelming for the team. That's why when you speak to someone engaged in an Agile program, it is not uncommon to hear, "The three weeks we tried it were the longest *eight* months of our lives." The repetition and relentless drive packs so much into daily life that things outside of the program feel ponderous. It's like traveling at warp speed at work and riding on a turtle the rest of the time.

For these and other reasons, when I encounter a company in need of a cultural change, I often turn to Agile-inspired techniques. Still, even when used at the right time, Agile can result in a disastrous outcome. For instance if leadership is not aligned about their culture, the approach may quickly result in the team running miles down the wrong path. Also, if everyone is running sprints (short burst, focused delivery cycles), there is not a lot of time for client interaction and the cultivation of creativity.

Making matters worse, I often have to rely on Agile techniques while the program is already moving 500 MPH at 30,000 feet. This means I need a mechanism for understanding the culture deeply and quickly so I can both know if Agile is the right tool but also help the team adapt to its rigor. Again, this is where identifying the forgotten pieces of an organization's culture (its *shmatas*) can be very powerful. Cultural artifacts can be used to create deeper, subconscious connections that help with alignment and acceptance of large-scale change at the root.

At the media company, I had to help them change how the organization approached work while quickly delivering results in a cost sensitive environment. Knowing time was of the essence I implemented the new function through one of my own Agile tools, the **Base Build**.

The Base Build is designed around an Agile concept known as the Minimally Viable Product or MVP for short. The idea behind the MVP is to bring a product or concept to the customer with the smallest number of features for viability or usability. In this way the customer is engaged sooner and can provide direct feedback before the team wastes energy on what may be the wrong features. Once the product is in use, it can then be quickly adjusted and enhanced. This approach forces development teams to move out of theoretical analysis quickly while engaging the customer sooner with a working concept they can touch and feel.

In this case, the Base Build was focused on implementing a new function with new processes, roles and responsibilities. This approach allowed me to draw up the processes in a matter of days and implement the new structure within a month. This was followed by a few weeks of testing, learning what worked and tweaking the process to perfection.

Standing up such an approach requires outstanding communication and trust across the team. This could only occur under such difficult circumstances because of the time I took to understand the people and their culture. By using their shmatas I was able to quickly break down barriers, build trust and create the right environment for change to be embraced. I also used the shmatas throughout the program as a mechanism to illustrate concepts. Like the time I used a song from one of the gold disks to bring home a point in a critical meeting. Small, subtle actions reinforced our budding trust and opened the team up to engaging in the process.

With the right transformational culture in place, we started to get things done in days instead of weeks and bypassed detailed, costly analyses.

Indeed, the newfound unity seized the attention of leaders around the globe in a way never seen before in the organization. Everyone wanted to be a part of our effort. We became the "go to" team for getting things done. And boy did we make a difference.

One day, the CFO asked if we could implement a new pricing program within the next month. After speaking with a few managers, it was apparent the team felt implementation would take an average of 6-9 months. When I relayed my conclusion to the CFO, he thanked me for my work and reiterated his desire for a one-month delivery.

Quite the conundrum!

In a flash, I turned to a favorite, but more extreme, Agile-based tool, the SWAT Team (a scrum team on steroids). In this construct, there is a **Scrum Master** who oversees the team's delivery through daily meetings (known as stand-ups) and reporting that is readily produced and delivered to management. Reporting is used throughout the effort to focus management on barriers that must be quickly removed for the team to proceed. The team is built around a singular focus or goal (sprint) that is delivered in a few weeks rather than months.

In this construct I replace Agile requirements or user stories with "to dos." Progress against the to dos are reviewed in brief, daily team meetings known as stand ups where the team provides terse updates on progress and any barriers that may require management intervention. The to do list is then rolled up at the end of week in a report to a governance team. This serves the dual purpose of engaging the customer (leadership) early and often and spreads the new way of working bottom up. This culture infects all who touch it and gets everyone rowing in the same direction fast.

A key difference in how I implement a scrum team vs. a traditional Agile coach is that I provide little to no training. Because we are all aligned at the core and it is more about the team than the tools, my teams figure things out in real time and are less afraid to learn through delivering, a.k.a. the Agile inspired concept of test and learn.[14] All I do is provide some initial guidance and the spark. I get the team stood up, create the initial tracker, run three or four meetings, and then hand off to the Scrum Master.

Once I hand over the controls, I disappear to avoid the disruption of my presence and influence. Agile is about empowering teams, not controlling or overtraining them. (Over training – particularly creating a team in your own image – will destroy the entire process.)

In the end, this resulted in full stand up of a new Agile work team with a real implementation plan in less than 72 hours. That's right – total rookies went from zero to top-end speed in three days! Ultimately, we blew the roof off the revenue goal and in under three weeks, created a new process that was repeated multiple times for even more benefit.

So, what's the downside of this SWAT Team method? Simple – it's only sustainable for two weeks, three weeks tops. People lose steam and rigidity dissolves everyone's spirits like acid eating away at tin. This is where the Transformation Lead really earns his pay. By keeping a watchful eye on the team as it cycles through the phases of transformation[15] – at any time, the Lead must be prepared to know when it's time to exit using this approach and switch to another. You disband the team because you have accomplished the goal – and you retire the tool until it is needed again.

The "rocket sled" heavy approach only worked because I had built trust at a foundational level and never did anything to lose it. I took time to know and relate to the members of the team through what really mattered. The company had been great once – there were still dedicated people who wanted to recreate the past glory that their shmatas embodied. The place had a culture of passion and success – all the folks needed was a spark of hope to rekindle the flames.

Look for artifacts – just as I did when I saw the stuff hanging on the wall. Pay attention to photos and plaques. Every office has them and while out of the way (sometimes), finding them does not require an Indiana Jones-like search. All it takes is a moment of sensitivity and you will soon be able to identify what I call an organization's "heritage-based culture." When you do, you will have unearthed the company's unique sauce and you will have the foundation of what you need to work together.

A final note on *shmatas*. They not only help you diagnose and understand but you can also use them as a powerful tool to establish new cultural norms.

Case in point: I was once leading a broad transformation for a leading financial services company. This project had it all: digital transformation, marketing modernization, sales centralization, outsourcing, creation of a new strategy function, and implementation of new IT infrastructure – the whole enchilada. You will hear a lot more about this project throughout the book but for now I want to mention one of the program's leaders who introduced me to something known as a "Challenge Coin." The military has a tradition of presenting coins as tokens to team members to signify comradery.

To keep his team motivated, the leader had a vendor make special, project-branded challenge coins. When he gave someone a coin, he explained its significance and talked about the tradition's place in the military.[16] We all proudly displayed our coins. No surprise – we delivered the farthest-reaching change in the company's history.

Even a few years later, I occasionally come across the coin and smile. The memento – though relatively inexpensive – is priceless and irreplaceable; it signifies my role in the culture of this company for many years to come.

So, the next time you feel lost in change, take a minute to stop and look around.

See if you can find an object that you identify with most.

What stories can you think of when you look at it?

Does the object anger you – or make you happy?

If it makes you unhappy, ask yourself why and what you need to do to change. Then go out, buy yourself a new shmata representing the change you seek and see what happens. You may find some exciting results that are even better than a long, hot shower on a Tuesday morning.

Key Takeaways:

- Each of us has a history and a story to tell. Sometimes we lose sight of things in the noise and can't find our way. This is where "shmatas" come in
- Shamatas are visible, cultural artifacts that can represent important sources of data about who we are and where we come from. They are easy to find if we only look
- When used with purpose, shmatas can be a powerful tool for establishing new norms
- Don't let getting started hold you back. You don't need perfection. Focus on the basics
  - o Create high level goals
  - o Establish a basic structure
  - o Stick to it

        o   Gather data

- As you go through your change journey don't forget to ALR (Act, Learn and Repeat) until you get it right

CHAPTER 3: THE DAY BILLY M. LOST HIS JOB

It was a sunny Sunday morning and I was around ten. I was full of life and couldn't wait to seize the day. As I popped out of bed, got dressed, and prepared to start my day with television and cereal, I was bombarded by my father demanding that I go to synagogue with him for Sunday morning services.[17]

Yeesh, I thought, *does this ever end?*

But like a good son, I got my belongings and went with him.

As the cantor labored on and boredom grew, I started listening to the surrounding gossip. Out of nowhere, someone turned to his friend and said, "Did you hear, Billy lost his job".

I had never spoken to Billy and I knew nothing about him but I sure as hell knew who he was. Billy was a serious looking man who was taller than most. He had a loud voice and a face that screamed, "Mess with me at your own risk." His children were clearly petrified of him and so was I.

Although I was a kid and did not know the family well, for some reason, the "tidbit" shook me to the core. I had never known anyone who lost their livelihood and I could not comprehend how things might work. I thought, *How could someone lose a job; aren't they permanent?*

To make matters worse, I was plagued with concern. What would happen to his family? How would Billy's children handle it? How would he pay for his home? How would his family eat? My mind raced. I was left shocked, scared, and dismayed all in a single breath.

Over the years I have revisited this event. To be honest, it has probably created some of the biggest challenges and successes for me. On the one hand, the sheer fear of losing a job always caused me to work harder. Fear of ending up like Billy has proven a great motivator.

On the other hand, this line of thinking was self-destructive. My fear of not having work, especially early in my career, is why I hopped around to so many jobs. I was so afraid of being typecast in a single niche that I was always looking for something new, something more interesting, something with more money, or something to make me more marketable in the inevitable event of a downturn.

I never developed depth in any subject or in any relationships. I was forced to rely on my sales skills and resume to get the next opportunity. In retrospect, while I was fortunate enough to find new jobs, my thinking stunted my career and limited my growth. Ironically, I probably would have had more stability had I stuck it out instead of becoming a "mile wide and an inch deep." Funny thing about bad thinking; it often results in the thing we are most trying to prevent.

Several years ago, I was leading a massive transformation for a leading financial services company. I was asked to lead the Project Management Organization (PMO)[18] which included five consultants overseeing almost two dozen work streams that ran the gamut from front to middle to back office. The client was looking to reduce costs, upscale technology, and minimize unpredictability by outsourcing operations to an integrated partner.

I worked night and day. We were way understaffed and no matter how much I complained to my partner and manager about needing an additional technology project manager support team, they would not listen. They were too afraid of the cost-conscious client and did not want to risk the job. Their answer was to push me and the team harder for months on end.

For the first nine months of my tenure I was *the* rock star.

Over the previous year there had been two other PMO leads, both of whom flamed out and left the project with a poor, heavy structure, and little momentum. I did what most do: I jumped in and started delivering heavy. I worked non-stop and carried the project forward almost single-handedly.

Months went on and the work began to take shape. We were delivering requirements and moving the ball down the field. I was invited to meetings with the senior most people, a big honor for someone like me at the time. Even with all the success, however, my undoing swooped in like a diving hawk snagging an unsuspecting field mouse.

My approach was unsustainable. The team was dying and not solely from the workload. The firm simply oversold its capabilities. I had never run anything even close to as large as this project at the time. When I mentioned my inexperience to the partner before I started, he said, "Don't worry; you will figure it out," which I did in the form of more administration, more bureaucracy, and more meetings.

The tipping point in my demise came from a very unlikely place: an internal audit. Unbeknownst to me, the company had specific guidance around artifacts and approaches for large initiatives. There was no way I was in line.

When the scathing audit report came out, I focused on damage control. But the Queen was already screaming, "Off with their heads!"[19] and I left the project rather quietly one Wednesday morning.

Funny thing – after I was history, the company established a central technology project management team under a new, more seasoned PMO leader – my recommendation from months earlier to a T.

A few months after my departure, I learned the project went live in record time and made a lot of careers. The client became a senior executive, my manager became a partner, and I was stuck in Nowheres-ville delivering a different, horrible project for a different, horrible, client.

For a long time, I was frustrated. I did not get any credit

– and, because I was replaced on the project, I thought I had failed. Even though I know the venture would have flown into the mountain without me, I felt slighted and angry. Feeling betrayed, I quit the firm a few months later.

I have reflected on this situation for a long time and arrived at a few conclusions. If I am making excuses, I can say that my partners did not support me because they were afraid of the client. Despite giving me an end-of-the-year award, they tossed me aside when it was convenient. The award was a control mechanism – a carrot to get me to work more without asking a lot of questions. Following the pattern of failure utilized by a lot of leaders and parents, my bosses did not want to find out how they could help or if they had done anything wrong.

In a more objective way, I think I failed because I did not fully understand the power of relationships or how to manage them. I was too focused on not letting anyone down for fear of losing my job when what I should have done was stop and use my relationships to help others understand why the current approach was futile. I opted instead for the quick satisfaction of "making first downs" over taking the time to build a proper foundation. I was simply too afraid of getting fired and acquiesced to the "move, move, move now" attitude. I was neither self-reflective nor confident enough to fight harder or differently for what was truly right: getting the team to work together on the right answer.

This fear haunted my entire time with large consulting firms. The companies I worked for were tops in the world with the best and brightest folks imaginable. Despite the talent and tools at my disposal, I could not reconcile my clients' needs with the firms' direction. Neither could I understand how to work for weeks on a deliverable with a client only to have a partner swoop in, trash my efforts, and then slither away. The partners were never in the trenches with me, so who were they to direct me?

Instead of understanding the structure and how the teams worked, I focused on billing more hours and doing more self-promotion when I should have used the power of the partners to my advantage. I was simply too afraid to try to interact for fear of being seen as incompetent. Instead, I kept working harder until there was no more gas in the tank.

Interestingly, I have learned over the years, from the thousands of people I have worked with, that I am not alone. Many folks have similar anxieties. Sometimes fear manifests in self-destructive behavior (like me); other times it presents as being disruptive to others. Think about times when "so and so is just such a jerk to work with." Is the person truly a jerk or just afraid of making a mistake?

On a similar project, I was once paired up with a day-to-day technology project manager. The gentleman had a reputation as "difficult." While I think he was "a little off," rather than having the confidence to do what I knew was right, I opted to make him happy. I feared that if he complained, everyone would listen, my imposter status would be exposed, and I would be fired.

For the first few months I busted my hump to make him happy. I endured endless meetings, nonsensical tirades and childish complaints. He sucked the hours out of my day with the efficiency of a Dyson. No matter what I delivered, making him happy resulted in a product that did not align with the boss's vision. I felt like an idiot searching for a village because all my ideas were "bad."

Over time I grew less able to manage the situation. One day the project manager's boss called me into his office to discuss "the noise." Instead of trusting my point of view, I bent over backwards to explain how we were, in fact, "working well together." I should have said, "This relationship is a disaster and here's why that guy should be handing out free samples at Walmart." I should have asked for some interventional counseling – some help in navigation. Maybe I could have engaged the PM more effectively. Instead, I handed the reins to my insecurities and said a lot of stupid stuff in defense of a guy who was undermining me as fast as he could work the shovel.

The moral of the story: change is hard, scary and always results in complex emotions. To be successful in transformation means having the confidence to not allow your fear to drive your decision making. By recognizing the emotions for what they are and focusing instead on understanding the transformation's vision and building relationships early on with your team, a transformation leader creates the right environment for delivering beyond insecurities.

Many years later, I heard Billy M.'s name again. He'd gotten a new job – then lost it. Wash. Rinse. Repeat. Apparently, he had a knack for the process. And yet, in the end, he retired to Florida a happy grandfather. Not bad for a miserable SOB.

Maybe he finally figured things out.

Maybe, like me, he needed to work for himself.

Or maybe he just got lucky.

Whatever the case, the day Billy M. lost his job changed my life.

But it does not rule me any longer.

Key Takeaways:

• Traumatic situations are an unfortunate part of life and can influence us in ways we don't al ways understand. Don't allow bad thinking to cause the thing you are trying to prevent
• Change is hard, scary and always results in complex emotions. Have the confidence to not allow fear to drive your decision making by rec ognizing the emotions for what they are
• The next time you are faced with fear, focus on understanding the vision and building good relationships. Act with purpose with your goals in mind and you will quickly find yourself on the right track

CHAPTER 4:
REFLECTIONS ON
MR. MANN

It was 1990 and I think I was in sixth grade. It was a great time. Guns N' Roses was the greatest band ever, nothing made me happier than playing dodgeball in gym class, and a soft vanilla ice cream cone with rainbow sprinkles from Carvel was the bee's knees. Yeah, life was good and most of all, simple.

Before the massive sharing machine that is the internet emerged, the only way to meet people and to disseminate information was – well – getting off your butt and meeting them to share stuff. In grade school there was no better place for camaraderie than the annual Science Fair. Sure, we learned what "weird Johnny" thought about the origins of the Universe, but the Fair also offered a chance to show off who we were, what we could do, and – with luck – take home the prize. The Science Fair gave me the opportunity to demonstrate I could hang – like my brother. But a bigger deal was the chance to impress my science teacher, Mr. Mann.

Mr. Mann was a clever guy. He understood efficiency in ways many managers only dream. For example, he brought automated Scantron[20] test grading technology to our little school. The tool allowed for quicker feedback/results and forever stopped the kid in the front row from waving his hand and asking, "Did you mark our quizzes yet?"

Even Mr. Mann's tests were the stuff of legend. Instead

of the usual multiple-guess extravaganzas, Mr. Mann devised efficient, single page gauntlets of multi-dimensional questions. The navigation provided not only entertainment but also genuine opportunities for learning. The type of questions varied – and there were always a few "freebies" or something funny. The mazes kept us on our toes and trained us to become better students and test takers.[21]

Naturally, Mr. Mann was the boss of the Science Fair; he determined who would win the coveted prize to compete at the "borough" level. As the day to pre-qualify ideas approached, my pre-adolescent mind geared up for the challenge. I wanted a winning topic.

Then – *Eureka!*

While I was playing Nintendo, my mother was nagging me about something. When she realized I was tuning her out, she burst into my room and, in classic sitcom fashion, grabbed me by the ear. My mother was tough, an elementary school science teacher in her own right (she went to the White House for a National Teacher Award or something), she was not an easy person to ignore.

As my lobe began to separate from the rest of my head, I wondered, *How did I tune her out?*

I realized the human mind cannot multitask – it gravitates to one thing or the other. Like water flowing downhill, the mind forces us to focus on the more interesting topic.

Cool, I thought once Mother released me from her death grip. *I need to test this.*

I did and, with my mother's help, I won the Science Fair at school and took first place in the borough competition.

Boo-yah!

More recently, I decided to retest this theory. One day while with a client, I noticed something. In large operations departments, without fail, there is always at least one person listening to a radio, usually "easy" music and always at low volume. Interestingly – the radio owner is often a valued member of the team in terms of morale, culture, and productivity.[22]

Maybe I was wrong, and it is possible to both walk and chew gum at the same time. In fact, maybe audio and visual stimuli boost productivity and should be encouraged.

Don't get me wrong; the idea is not novel. Investment banks have been placing very high earners at desks (rather than cubicles or offices) for generations. These super high energy, productive workers are surrounded by ringing phones, CNN, Bloomberg, and countless other "distractions." Someone a heck of a lot smarter than me figured this out long ago. But, as you move to more operational roles, this type of environment is less common. In most Operations Centers, you can hear heartbeats as time marches inexorably along and increasing numbers of workers entertain ideas of running off to Peru just to escape the seconds thumping away. So, maybe we could improve culture in operation centers by encouraging the right audio and visual stimuli?

One day on the client's site I decided to test this theory. I pulled out my neon blue running headphones and listened to music – *my* music: Daft Punk, Led Zep, and Avicii. I rocked out – and might even have danced a little.[23] Before you laugh, I not only burned calories, but it also gave me the energy to work harder and longer.

More recently I had the good fortune of working for a client that offered ergonomically designed desks. You know the desks that rise up so you can stand and work. Add in a more casual work environment and I can now work in running shoes. And I am better than ever. Even with my new noise cancelling DJ headset, I never miss someone coming up to talk to me. My productivity is through the roof and I am happier during the day. I go home in a better mood where the morale has improved. This, has made things better at home and you know what they say… happy wife, happy life![24]

I took this learning a step further when building my home office. When I first started out and thought I needed to become the next Big 4 consultant, I rented space from a well-known office sharing company. Don't get me wrong, the place was super cool, but I was paying $400 a month for an office that I visited once every ninety days – at most.

I have come to understand better what makes me tick and opted instead to use the money to create a great workspace at home. Tapping into my creative juices, I went a little crazy and embarked on a mission to craft the perfect, high-tech sensory experience. I invested in a very nice computer and monitor and purchased a special light fixture that allows me to lower the visual temperature in the room with the turn of a knob.

I bought a surround sound system – installed it myself: two Bluetooth speakers that link up with the push of a couple of buttons. For those especially busy times (or times of high distraction – like being on a plane), I snagged a very nice noise cancelling headset.

At lunch, I do yoga (my own mat and everything) and use a high-density roller. I stand at my desk on an ergonomic mat and have a neck massager for those hard days. When I need to sit, I plop into an ergonomic, reclining CEO chair like the ones you see on *Silicon Valley.*

I eliminated soda and went on a healthy, whatever I want in moderation diet. My senses are alive to the slightest hint of flavor. It is amazing.

To keep from overwhelming my nose – or other people's – I got odor absorbing gels and a time-release, scented spray. I have a fan and a small heater – always have proper air circulation.

While this investment seems excessive, consider the results. After installing my office, I worked from home for two months straight. Not a week went by where I did not put in at least a few hours a day every day. Most days began at 7:30 AM and ending at nearly 11:00 PM. I complete things I had always delayed – like this book.

To get a sense of just how productive, I have worked with virtually no vacation for the last twelve months and I am only now a little burned out. I have downtime on the weekends (I work a little), for religious reasons, and during traditional holidays but I am never idle. I have rediscovered my love of the outdoors – swimming, hiking, biking, and – wait for it – learned how to play the harmonica. My chill time is busy but gives me inspiration to reflect on my job and how I can improve, all of which makes me better. You want a recipe for worker longevity and productivity, here it is… just add a dash of music and let employees have the freedom to be themselves.

From a productivity perspective, my relatively small investment saved me money and represents one of the best decisions I ever made. If I need to meet with a client, I go to them. When I entertain, I do it here.

My science project suggested stimuli are bad but then how could they be so good? I am thinking it may be time to tell Mr. Mann I was wrong and – gasp – return my trophy.

In truth, I realize now that my sixth-grade hypothesis was only partially right. Yes, stimuli can be disturbing, but they can also be helpful if used properly. The key is to identify the stimuli and customize them to the desired behavior. In this way stimuli can actually help you do a better job. Again, not a novel conclusion[25] and yet, many companies still do nothing about it. A seemingly small fix, like adding a television with news to an operation center, may pay for itself in productivity gains many times over and yet you are more likely to find a clock endlessly ticking and sounding like, "Buehler, Buehler, Buehler."[26] By embracing "work from home" for employees like me, companies can hope to realize real dollar savings in terms of lower occupancy rates[27] and increased efficiency from people working in environments tailored to them. Just let people be themselves rather than trying to control every aspect of their environment. Trade monotony for a focus on stimuli that encourage thinking and flexibility and the results will speak for themselves.

Even when a dramatic change seems so hard, small changes to stimuli can go a long way.

Don't believe me?

Try painting a room in your house?

Or the next time you feel bad, put on some new clothing.

The next time you feel lost, try something small and see what happens. That small change could be the spark to something much bigger.

Mr. Mann taught me a lot about life. He showed me that in anything we do, there are always opportunities to do what we do better if we are brave enough to try. Mr. Mann never laughed at me when I created a science project in the 1980's with "Nintendo" in the title. His approach to learning gave me the courage to make the idea of encouraging individuality a foundational element of a philosophy that has helped billion-dollar companies the world over. (Even if it means a funny looking guy wearing blue exercise headphones and flashy running sneakers,) My science teacher gave me the confidence to be myself and to enable others to do the same.

Mr. Mann, if you are still out there, thanks.

Key Takeaways:
- Great leaders don't try to control people. They empower them to be themselves
- Stimuli in our environments can be powerful mechanisms for driving change. With a little practice, you can identify these stimuli and cus tomize them to drive you or your teams behavior

Section 2: Soul

A young person's entering adulthood has a lot of similarities to a company experiencing growth. First, strange things start to happen. You start seeing odd things in odd places. *Should that be there?* You feel weird. Emotional baggage piles like the dirty clothes on your floor and someone – you or your mom – is likely going to melt down at any moment. As you grow, you need to stretch...expand. Despite anecdotal evidence to the contrary, most kids don't want to live at home forever. Our curiosity leads us to look for new friends and new circles of influence. We find new stimuli – different ideologies from those driven home by parents and custom. Although sometimes with reluctance, we receive feedback and criticism. We craft a style and learn how to market ourselves.

It's not often easy, and not often kind but most of us exit the tube at the other end of the journey to adulthood a little bruised, but intact.

Emerging mid-market companies experience similar growing pains. Where once you did one thing (investing in sales or product quality), now you face the reality of spending money on core infrastructure. You have more reserves than before, but you cannot afford to burn cash on something that will not add *pop.*

In the long run, most of us succumb to the advice of the old adage, "fake it till you make it." We all try to look tough and hope no one punches us in the mouth (either literally or meta-phorically). We know there is always a schoolyard bully lurking out there, someone with deeper pockets and a burning desire to kick every little guy's ass.

Before I became an entrepreneur, I felt like a teenager trapped in a growing young man's body. I didn't know who I was, and I only thought I knew what I wanted. In some ways, I did a lot better than I thought. After all, successful marriages are harder to come by every day. But in others, I felt like I was a disaster.

Let's consider a word we all know and hate: *failure.*

What does it mean to be a failure?

Is it a matter of wealth?

Is it something to do with family?

Is it, attitude?

For me it's a mix. Wealth provides a means to an end. I don't need a fancy car or a spectacular house. I just want enough money to feel safe. I want to know my family can survive an economic meltdown without sacrificing our quality of life – to be happy with what I have (which means: enough).

All interconnected.

Without a feeling of contentedness, one tends to grasp, tread water, and – if you are not careful – to sink.

This was especially true for me early on in my career when I felt limited by the quality of my higher education. I did poorly in high school, and it was a wonder I got into college at all. For a long time, I was bitter about my shortcomings and blamed my college for the challenges I encountered when I looked for my first job.

Even when I got a B.S. and a master's, I was not fulfilled. The school I went to was not good enough. I had to go to an Ivy, or the sheepskin meant nothing.

I eventually lived my dream – and the experience is everything they say. The quality of the instructors, the feel of the program, the academic openness – very cool. And, when I entered the business world, the name at the top of the diploma helped – but there were no guarantees.

Plenty of kids in my graduating class had difficult times finding work and staying employed. The world is cutthroat and an Ivy helps for about five minutes. This led to new ideas of what "more" looked like until I was back on the hamster wheel.

Understanding what you want is hard; it's no different when companies set goals. Whether the goals are for a project, employee, merger, or even the mission/vision statement of a startup, while everybody knows they need to set goals of some sort, they often end up with an unintended result. While this is not always a bad thing, it can often be hard to adjust to the changes along the way. This is where The Simpel Kinetic Transformation Philosophy's focus on flexibility comes into play. If everything went as planned, we would all be Warren Buffet. Our ability to adjust and flex as a change occurs determines whether we are successful on the other end. This means knowing where you want to go is of course important but the only way to get there is to know when to take the shortcut and when to stay on the long, yellow brick road. It is often within the earliest and most widely accepted tasks, like setting goals and turning them into meaningful action, that the seeds for so many future problems lie.

Consider a typical high-technology, new product development cycle at a Fortune 500. Even today, most projects are run with a Waterfall method or hybrid Agile process. "The business" defines what it requires and communicates the needs with the IT and Operations teams. Better organizations work together to "solution" the requirements into what is known as "functional requirements." IT uses these detailed, process-heavy documents to create the IT portion of the product for testing with users.

While to the layperson this approach may seem logical, it often results in massive rework. Teams are operating in a "pass the baton fashion" where no one sees the big picture until the end. Then, when changes occur, the team needs to go deep to execute even small fixes.

The Agile methodology was created to combat this very problem. However, even when Agile is employed properly, the transparency and drive it creates often clashes with those operating at a more traditional pace. The result: the initial goals for the project become bogged down in communication issues and reconciling what was desired from what was delivered.

The lack of connection between proper goal setting and execution is a critical issue in today's fast-moving corporate world but it also impacts us on a personal level. For example, ask a fifteen-year-old what he wants to be, and you are likely to get an answer like, "A billionaire of course."

I mean – why not. I don't think most middle teens will say, "A mid-level employee with a wife, three kids, another one on the way, two mortgages, $50,000 in unsecured debt, a snowball's chance in hell of advancement, season *Knicks* tickets, and a borderline alcohol problem." No, kids aim big and want to follow their dreams – that is until they get lost in life, veer off course, and then wake up one day wondering how their lives ended up the way they did.

So why does this happen?

Of course, there are lots of reasons but the one I want to focus on is the idea of trying to do too much. Rather than zeroing in on creating a simple vision with attainable goals and then acting towards achieving them in a flexible, collaborative fashion, companies, like people, often get lost in minutiae.

The best companies I have worked with understand and use goal setting as a collaborative process where the first focus is on high level alignment and immediate action over long-winded strategic proposals. The immediate action is couched in a broader plan that bends and flexes fluidly as the transformation demands. Knowing this, I can always tell within seconds whether a transformation will fail. All I do is stand face to face with a senior leader and ask, "What goal are we trying to achieve?" If there is any misalignment or doubt at the basic level, I know that no matter how talented the leader, he/she will not succeed. Without alignment on big stuff the small stuff does not matter.

To this end, I always use the first few days of any project to force very uncomfortable and specific conversations about goals, what measurable success looks like, and the projects the company will use to get there. Like I said earlier, most of the time the answer is staring us right in the face. Sometimes we don't realize it and we are just too afraid to ask. This is why the philosophy's focus on Fearless Honesty throughout the program is so critical. Yeah, it can be hard but if used properly and persistently, you can avoid more costly headaches. This is especially true up front when goals are under construction and early execution can mean the difference between going right or left.

Sure, I am unflinching and direct, but I don't wait for perfection to begin. Rather, I start pressing work at the same time I am building the details. In this way, we line up all the way through delivery, which allows us to test and learn the goals together. The key is not to shy away from the questions but to make them part of the process. As success mounts, instead of feeling they have been overloaded, people have a sense of ownership and the confidence to swing harder.

Once I have my hypotheses around the goals, I begin implementing the most basic governance structure I can establish (a Base Build). Again, keeping it simple, I focus on nothing more than decision making and accountability. In this way, the very people who need to help define the goals are the ones who own the delivery. For those less familiar with a typical corporate program governance structure, it may include:

- Identifying key stakeholders and getting to know them,
  - Forming a leadership team known as a Steering Committee to own decision making,
- Organizing work into manageable bodies,
- Consistent, frequent, structured touchpoints
- Developing kick off materials that result in actionable next steps,
- Tracking and managing results through data and reporting.

This is also where once again the pre-work around understanding the culture comes in very handy. Using my understanding of the environment together with actively facilitating the governing body that can do something with the information, I quickly remove barriers to decision making and get the team working together.

Another technique I also use up front during goal setting is known as personal relative estimation.[28]

I learned this technique observing my father doing math.

Growing up, I was always fascinated with how quickly my dad could solve an equation. Now, I'm not talking about quadratic equations or anything like that but still... give him any two numbers to multiply and within an instant you have an answer.

Over the years I learned that my father never really got it right but he came so close no one questioned. And to be honest, it was more than sufficient. What he clued in on was, people sometimes get so lost in precision that they lose the spirit of the question; to get an answer!

To move quickly, my father would break the numbers down into something divisible by ten and then estimate the rest. He was so close, so often that everyone, even to this day is still amazed by his speed.

Realizing the power of estimation, I too created my own method. My realization working with companies is people struggle so much with embarrassment that they much more often than not, burn calories on getting a precise answer that isn't even precise or easily understood.

For example, say you get an 85 out of 100 on a test. You might think that is a B and if you are an over-achiever, you would be upset. Now, what if I told you that you got the highest grade in the class, the next closest grade was a 70 and the teacher is going to employ a curve, giving you an A?

Business works like this as well. We don't really know, especially early on, the context for analysis. People get lost in the blue skies of the abstract and wind up burning valuable capacity on needless analysis. By finding personal examples to make the numbers more accessible, I help teams quickly get over this hump. Again, my examples are specific and grounded in my client's culture. This leads to acceptance and much more sticky learning than typical, consultant heavy approaches.

This technique also helps speed decision making because the estimates are quick and 9 out of 10 times prove to be largely accurate. The idea here is to organize work as quickly as possible. The bias to "just get started" even with imperfect information helps the team start delivering results right away with speed and efficiency. This approach allows me to test my hypotheses with real data, learning if they are accurate and then collaboratively adjusting my approach in real time along the way. Simple, common sense, I know, but you would be shocked how often people spend extraordinary amounts of time and money trying to figure out a root cause instead of allowing the action and results to drive validation of their ideas.

When I was young, I didn't really understand what I wanted out of a career. It took me over two decades to discover I was an entrepreneur.

But I was much luckier in the "love and life" department.

When I met my wife, we clicked – physical, personal, and goals. Whenever we spoke about life and a future together, we always synced up around what we wanted in terms of religion, children, and our way of life. Some things have changed, but as we continue to work together, we get stronger and more aligned by the day. Even after almost 25 years!

What made our life work was that we didn't need to wait to figure it all out. When we clicked, we were willing to work together to iron out the details. Yes, it got tough, but we never gave up because we were running on parallel tracks. For us, it is as simple as that.

By focusing on the big things, like having the right general goals and a bias for action, even when I failed, I always failed up - it has made all the difference in life and my career too.

Key Takeaways:

- Not taking the proper time up front to set goals and create alignment are often key reasons for failure during times of change
- Throughout a change, it is important to constantly revisit your goals and understand how your actions support your aims

- Especially early on, it is more important to create a simple vision with attainable goals then trying to flesh everything out to the lowest level of detail. Remember "ALR"
- Goal setting should be a collaborative process with a focus on alignment and immediate action over long-winded strategic proposals. Immediate action couched in a plan that promotes flexibility as you respond to change is a key to success
- Don't be afraid to estimate, especially early on. You may be closer than you think
- Estimates should be personal and relatable. Again, it is about alignment over details. The rest comes through execution

CHAPTER 5:
LISTENING TO
THE BIRDIES

One of my favorite people in the world was my mother-in-law, God rest her soul.

Diane grew up in a small town in South Africa. She met her husband at the hospital where they worked. He served as a pediatrician; she was a nurse.

Over the course of their marriage, Diane and Abraham produced three children and lived an amazing life together. They spent a few years in Canada while my father-in-law pursued advanced medical study. Then, they returned to South Africa for a while. Sensing they might never encounter the right opportunities, Diane and Abraham were fortunate enough to gain entry to the United States. Here, in middle America, my father-in-law blossomed. Inspired by a rabbi and lifelong friend to this day, Abraham embraced his heritage and found meaning in his life.

While life proved pleasant, the couple decided to relocate once again – this time to the north east. With Abraham ensconced at a leading university hospital and medical school, Diane settled in as a school nurse.

My in-laws prided themselves on living in a simple way with clear views about materialism, faith, tradition, and (most of all) family. Their strength and courage in the face of adversity and the challenges all immigrants face earned them the admiration of the entire community. With a love that would make Buttercup and Westley[29] jealous, they honored one another, their neighbors, and their community.

While my in-laws were a lot of things, big spenders was not one of them. Perhaps it was their desire for simplicity and for substance over form. Maybe they never quite acclimated to an alien economic environment. Whatever the reason, they never lived lavishly. In fact, Abraham still sits in the same lounge chair he occupied forty years ago. He doesn't want to change it because, "It reminds me of my family."

'Nuff said.

My wife – and I say this with all certainty that I will pay dearly for it – must have skipped these core life lessons from her parents. Although neither high maintenance nor ostentatious, she loves her some elegance. Have you ever seen an intergenerational group of *yentas* form a WhatsApp group discuss the royal family? I have.

With these competing viewpoints in mind, you might imagine some legendary fights about things financial between Sara and her folks. Not so. Their disagreements were so few and far between that they can remember every detail of every one of them years later. As far as I know, Sara and Abraham had two brouhahas: 1) a Debbie Gibson hat; 2) pants under a skirt.

Fini.

However, like all things, no one is perfect and apparently things really got out of hand one time.

It was the early 1990s and like most kids, my wife went with her mother to the local mall.

"Mom, can I have this new dress?" Sara asked with (I'm sure) all the sugar and spice I have come to know and love.

To her dismay Diane was having none of it.

"Put that back" she said, "and find something less expensive.".

In a flash, my wife said something she regrets to this very day.

"You know what the birds say when they fly over our

house, cheap, cheap, cheap…"

Ka-boom!

Although the story seems rather simple, it taught me one of the most important lessons in life: don't ever sweat the small stuff. Perfection – in a person or a relationship – is a myth. As we grow older with one another, we learn how to prioritize what irritates us – what sets us off – what we will accept. We save the fighting for items of true importance. Some call it, "compromise" – others say, "survival." Either way, it's all about the importance of lining up on what really matters. The rest is just commentary.

Sadly, it took me over forty years to get it. Like most young men with big ambition, early on in my career I was abrasive. I thought I knew best about – well – pretty much everything and I let everyone know. In truth, I was too cocky to realize what should frighten me.

My job involves high intensity, high visibility, and a need to prove value every second of every day. I deliver programs against tight deadlines and often with specific expectations (like "Save x% in year 1" or "Increase revenues by $y"). It's hard

No whining – just the facts – it's hard.

Nowhere was my challenge striking this balance clearer than during my earliest roles as a project manager.

For those who may not know: "project management" involves organizing teams, opening communication, and using tools like budget files to oversee a project and ensure everyone knows what to expect and when. As part of the role, the Project Manager owns the escalation and shepherding of risks and issues to resolution. If you do nothing else, a successful Project Manager is measured most in her ability to identify, communicate and facilitate resolution of risks and issues standing in the way of a program's success.

Before I developed my transformational approach, getting someone to meet a deadline included multiple calls, emails, and conversations. I often got the results, but my annoyance level ratcheted to an extreme volume over the life of a project. Believe me when I tell you I would not have won any "Most Popular" awards. My recipe did not guarantee either success or quality – and eventually caught up with me.

Taking the time to build relationships based on the essential things – your goals – when you are delivering a complicated change program is vital. Emotions run high and the last thing anyone wants is a transformation lead who adds to the stress by just not getting it. However, even when you are new and unsure of yourself, when goals are simple and clear, it's funny how things work out and people align. The big stuff is truly what matters. The rest, is of course, commentary.

Goal setting is about more than just setting the goal. It is also about implementation and tracking how you deliver against these goals. If done properly, the simple step of capturing your progress along the way, such as in a journal, can provide a fertile ground for maintaining alignment, delivering specific, action-oriented feedback and frankly helping you overcome anxiety.

Proper tracking against goals is a simple idea everyone knows and yet so few of us do. Study after study shows that you are far more likely to accomplish something if you write it down. Best of all, you don't need a master's degree, just the habit.

For me, on any project I create a simple task sheet with the following headers:
- Task name
- Category (what goal the task aligns to)
- Owner (who owns delivery of the task)
- Due date
- Status (red, yellow or green)

I have seen more "sophisticated" project managers do a lot more but, in the end, the above 5 items are really all you need to get control of everything from daily life to a $100 million dollar transformation at a global Fortune 500. Once you have the control, you can track as much as you like. The idea is to ensure traceability and alignment and to recognize when you are veering off course. Sometimes that's ok and you adjust accordingly. The key, is to know.

Over time, as the large and small wins add up, you gain something many of us don't often have, perspective. Because the datasheet is simple to maintain, it can be manipulated to look for trends. Together with the collective knowledge learned from goal setting and execution, this indicative data becomes another powerful tool to round out early assumptions, build momentum and deliver grounded feedback.

Perspective is something Diane instilled in my wife and has in turn translated to me. Sure we fight but we always come together about the big things. There is no confusion about what our goals are and they provide structure as we execute in our day to day lives.

Think about yourself or your company. Do you know what your goals are? Can you do a quick inventory of how your actions helped or hindered your goals? So often we get lost in the day to day that it becomes easy to lose sight and we end up wasting time on things that don't really matter. Of course, sometimes this is good, such as when you are having fun, but during times of focused transformation, the leader must never allow the team to go far astray. Easy, quick stand up of data is the best way I have found to do this.

Thinking about Diane always makes me so proud and, of course, sad. She stood for so many important things. Even years after her death, people remember her for her big ideas and actions.

Diane taught me never to be afraid to test and learn because if you focus on what really matters, you can overcome anything – even the loss of someone special.

Key Takeaways:

- Remember the old adage: don't ever allow yourself to sweat the small stuff. Perfection is a myth

- Always be sure to build relationships based on commonality, particularly when it comes to goals. Revisit the goals together throughout the program to ensure you are aligned
- Success often lies in taking the time to con sciously capture data. It doesn't have to be hard or complex and over time even small data adds up and can tell a profound story

CHAPTER 6: SIMPEL

At last, I am up to the part where I talk about the most important relationship and the most important person in my life: my wife.

I met Sara when I was 18 years old in late April. I was wearing dark green sweatpants, a white tee-shirt, and a baseball cap. My wife was wearing a white Banana Republic tee-shirt with a long black skirt, and black sweatpants underneath. Her shoes had light blue emblems on the sides. I remember how the sun made her golden blonde hair glisten. It was truly love at first sight.

At least for me.

When I was younger, I was shy and awkward. The issue only got worse around women. Imagine the horror of seeing the love of your life and being too afraid to follow her.

As I planned my move, a friend walked by and started a conversation. In the middle of our chat, Sara walked past. My friend gave her a hug, turned to me, and said, "Moshe (my Hebrew name), this is my friend Sara. Now you be nice to her."

Sara moved on – I grew weak in the knees. I was sad to let her get away but could not bring myself to risk any pursuit.

I failed to mention we were in Israel – a Passover holiday program at various *kibbutzim*. I spent the next three days trying to get transferred to the one where Sara stayed.

Bzzzzzzt! "Nope. They have enough *boys;* you'll mess up the ratio."

After the program ended and we went back to our seminaries, I feared I would never see Sara again. A sense of doom settled over me, and I kicked myself for not acting. I had not even tried.

Why?

Salvation came from an unexpected source.

My roommate and I did not get along and we were not friends. But one day, he asked me and another friend if we wanted to go with him to meet his girlfriend. Maybe he wanted the company; more likely, he wanted to split cab fare.

Either way – we went.

He met his girlfriend at a reunion of the *kibbutz* where Sara had stayed. The minute I walked in I heard her intoxicating laugh. Then, I saw the infectious smile. I would never have done anything, but the only available seat in the overflowing restaurant was – yes, thank you, God – next to Sara.

Over the course of the night, I might have said, "Pass the salt." Kicking myself, I decided this would never happen again. But before I could take any proactive stance, I heard something that still makes me shudder.

Another guy at the event had taken a shine to "my Sara." Unlike me, he was not afraid to act. "Sara Milner – very cool," he said, and, to my chagrin, he asked my roommate for her number.

My friend took Sara out multiple times. Although Sara claims they did not "date" but "went on dates,"[30] I was still very sad.

I was sure I had blown my only chance at happiness.

Making matters worse, not an hour before my friend made his move "not to date my wife," I had told another friend that I had met the girl I was going to marry.[31]

After close to a month of what my friend was sure was a mutually blossoming relationship, he stopped by my room. "Tonight," he said, "I'm asking Sara to be exclusive."

He might as well have punched me in the stomach.

Trying not to vomit, I asked, "She into you?"

"Wouldn't any girl be?" he replied and waltzed out.

To my splendid surprise, the Titanic had a better night. He could barely talk about it when he returned to school on Monday.

"She's not as into me as I am to her," is about all he said.

After that, I only saw Sara one more time in Israel – at a frozen yogurt shop. Though I tried to summon the courage to talk to her, it was no use. She was reminiscing with all her friends – I was a fifth wheel. Next thing I knew, Sara was on a plane back to America.

After sulking for days – and questioning my manhood – I boarded a plane for home. Once we were in the air, I swear the pilot slowed down on purpose.

**

I spent the remainder of the summer as a lifeguard at a well-known sleep away camp. Back then, I looked pretty good: thin and athletic with muscular arms, shoulders, and legs. I had a rebellious, contrarian personality – college kids thought I was okay.

We had a sort of "field day" competition. I was on the rowing team, something at which I excelled. Except...

...I had an asthma attack and nearly lost consciousness.

Refusing any help, I slunk away to the Nurse's Office.

A lovely nurse attended to me. When I could finally breathe without gasping, I noticed her accent. "Where are you from?" I asked.

"South Africa."

Without thinking, I said, "Is your daughter Sara Milner?"

She recoiled like I'd hit her with a jolt of electricity.

"How did you know that?" she asked.

My response?

"Fate."

**

A few months later I was in college and focused. I avoided social contact and zeroed in on my studies. One night, one of my roommates dragged me along when he went to visit his girlfriend (and to double date with one of her friends). As we dropped the young lady at her dorm, I saw Sara – my Sara – walking along. She looked beautiful and sophisticated. When she saw us, she came over to talk because – are you ready – my blind date was her roommate.

Sometimes Fate drops a piano on your head. I finally got it – I was meant to be with this woman. Given my monk-like attention to my studies, my roomie was stunned when I offered to go back with him to see his girl. I made sure Sara was included in the festivities.

We spent the entire evening talking. She was (and is) as beautiful on the inside as she is stunning on the surface.

She was smart, traditional, outspoken, and self-assured. I knew I was in love.

At the end of the evening, I beat my internal anxiety into submission and asked what she was doing the next weekend.

"Going to Staten Island."

"I'll be there too – at my parents' house," I responded. "How about I give you a ride back to the City on Sunday?"

Dr. Evil[32] should be so cunning. I gave her my number – (Good Guy 101 – "she'll never suspect your real motive") – then spent the entire weekend praying she would call.

When she did and asked for a ride, I immediately jumped into action.

I lied.

"Dad needs the car,"

Truth is, I never had access to a car. I had been casting for an excuse to see and talk to her. I apologized like someone who'd murdered a bunny rabbit, then – my linguistic gymnastics depleted – said goodbye.

The instant I got back to my dorm, I got Sara's number and called to apologize. She was delightful and unvengeful. Then, with a last, heroic effort, I popped the question.

"To make up for the lack of a ride, would you like to go to the movies?"

She said *yes!*

At the end of our third date, I finally worked up the courage to let Sara in on the secret and said, "Sara, I am very sensitive and scared of rejection. So, I avoid overcommitting and potentially getting hurt. So, what if, hypothetically, I asked you to be my girlfriend?"

Twenty-two years later, I still have her number.

I am a very lucky man. As the years have gone on, most of the people I know who married young ended up divorced or worse, in a loveless marriage. I cannot imagine anything more horrid than waking up every day next to someone I want to flee.

People stay in bad situations for a variety of reasons: social/familial pressure, financial considerations, laziness, the kids. I would probably do the same. Given my rakish good looks (gag) and winning personality, if I went back on the market, I'd probably be snatched up in a mere decade or three. The thought terrifies me.

We all have reasons for maintaining the status quo – even when we hate it – and no one from the outside has a right to judge us. Each person must make his/her own decisions and do the best he/she can.

I think Sara and I have plowed through despite the challenges life has thrown at us because we both wanted it as much as the other. And therein lies the key message.

When we were dating, Sara and I must have broken up 100 times. In retrospect, we were children who thought we knew it all. I probably "pulled the plug" more often than she did, but, honestly, my actions stemmed from fear. On the occasions Sara said she had enough of me, I always called her and pleaded for her to take me back. In the end, we pushed past anger, frustration, and hurt to make a home.

She has endured my business career wherever it took me because no matter what, we were always in agreement about where we ultimately wanted to go. After twenty plus years of failing up, I realized one day that I had enjoyed the good fortune of working in more industries and for more leading firms than anyone else I have ever known or met. This led to my epiphanies and the book you are holding today.

I wish I were the type of person who found what he was looking for easily, what he was good at doing, and then lived happily ever after. But like all perfect things in life, it is rarely true. I'm not a guy who will put in 10-20 years, rise through the ranks, then hover in the Purgatory of middle management until an arbitrary corporate downsizing move led by some jerk who has never met me (and does not want to) takes me out at the knees. And still, Sara hung in there.

I put my wife and family through hell while I wandered through the quagmire of self-discovery. To this day, I am sorry about the people I let down as I pursued the happiness I dreamt about every time I closed my eyes. Luckily for me, my wife and family always prioritized what was important and were willing to test and learn while we worked out the details together.

Things are similar for the Transformation Lead. Sometimes, especially when projects are underway, the team is foaming at the mouth, and it is easy to get bogged down, fatigued, or frustrated. What makes the Transformation Lead unique is the ability to find ways to hold onto the commitment to see everything through – to utilize every interaction as an opportunity for something meaningful and positive. But most of all it is the ability to inspire faith in the team that things will work out if everyone works towards the common goals.

For the rest of her life, Diane continually asked me how I knew she was Sara's mother. After all, I was lying on the exam table and wheezing to the point of unconsciousness.

Though I was haughty, I was also sheltered and, despite my travels, unworldly. I'm not sure I knew there was a *South* Africa, and I promise you I could not have found it on a map. Not only was Sara the only person I'd ever met from the country I didn't know about, she was also the only Jewish person from said mystical land. Ergo (and I promise I will *not* use "ergo" again in this book), any Jewish woman from South Africa old enough to be *my* mother must have been Sara's mother.

Sometimes it is good to take a chance on important things and to let fate do the rest. You never know when your leap of faith will result in a great story to tell your grandkids.

Key Takeaways:

- Relationships are about building mutual dedi cation. If you are both not in it at a fundamental level, all the fluff won't matter
- Never forget to prioritize what is really im portant and don't be afraid to test and learn. The details will work themselves out
- Every interaction is an opportunity for some thing meaningful and positive
- Sometimes it is good to take a chance on im portant things and to let fate do the rest

CHAPTER 7: THREE-FOR-THREE DOESN'T JUST HAPPEN

Two of my favorite people are my cousin Jane and her husband John. Both Jane and John are accomplished doctors, parents, and humanitarians. They are successful and modest. Each gives back to the community and is dedicated to their families – good people; you would like them.

One day I had the opportunity to enjoy a Saturday lunch with John's parents. After spending over thirty years in Long Island, they'd bought a house in Florida. They are "snowbirds."

As we chowed down on one of Jane's five main courses, I got to know John's mother, Frances. Like any good mother, Frances was more than happy to share the story of her family with me.

Frances is the daughter of Holocaust survivors. I am always astounded by the resiliency and success of "The Greatest Generation."[33] Imagine being betrayed by your country, losing everything, and shuffling into "work camps" to watch your friends and family members starved, tortured, and murdered.

None of the survivors I meet come across as broken. They have made a life for themselves and their children and children's children. From my grandmother (who grew up during Mao Zedong's Cultural Revolution in China) to Frances' parents who survived the Nazi camps, every individual radiates a miraculous faith and strength. Those heroes deeply impact everything in my life.

Frances' parents arrived in the United States with the shirts on their backs and gratitude to still have their lives. Though impoverished, they maintained rich and vibrant spirits; they dedicated themselves to what was left of their family. With a mother and father still reeling from the atrocities of the war and little to no help, Frances pursued her love of learning and carved out a career as a teacher. With her husband Hank (also an educator), she reared three children in the greater New York City area. They faced the difficulties of long hours, low pay, and underappreciation. Observant Jews, they wrestled with the financial pressures of private education for their kids and the social challenges of keeping kosher.

Interesting – I have never heard their son, John, mention anything about a difficult childhood. When he speaks of his younger years, it is always in terms of happiness and warm memories. He loves Frances and Hank – a sentiment they thoroughly return.

Talk about a Hallmark family. All three of Frances and Hank's children are beautiful, happily married, and professionally successful. They are all quite involved in their communities, schools, and their children's lives. Really amazing people – I am proud to have them as relatives.

Sitting at dinner, I realized I had a golden opportunity to pick the brain of one of the greatest managers of all time. Frances' success in overseeing and "manufacturing" a trio of magnificent offspring meant something – surely, she had a system.

"What's the secret?" I asked.

Instead of resorting to "Ah shucks, it was all luck," this modest, self-effacing woman smiled and said, "You do know that three-for-three doesn't just happen." (John still does not believe she said it because the comment is totally out of character. Guess what? She said it.)

We laughed and I realized Frances faced the same challenges we all do as parents. Of course, her son, John, wanted to be a garbage man at one point and actively petitioned his parents for permission to leave his expensive private school. Indeed, her daughters also spoke of their own, youthful, low-bar goals – and admitted they caused their share of trouble. But such are the pitfalls of youth.

From our conversation it became clear that like many other successful leaders, Frances and Hank's parenting was grounded in a set of wholesome guiding principles – you know them when you see them. The more I think about it, all good parents I know seem to have similar ideas. Maybe they don't even realize it but they all do and seem to have their own lexicons to explain their principles to boot. For example, my father-in-law calls it, "The Gold Standard." A set of solid lines that cannot be crossed no matter what.

Standard	Principle
There is no fail only not trying	Accountability
Only "I" can do it	Accountability
Dream big	Vision
Religion and family	Consistency
Know when to listen	Risk Management
It takes so little to cause harm and so much to cause good	Risk Management
Family first, always	Transparency
Never lose faith even when questioning	Transparency

These principles are more than rules. They are instinctive guiding principles geared towards building a good life. The concepts are not secret, but they are unyielding. Anything less is unacceptable.

As we have seen, transformation is complicated and confusing. Emotions can cloud our judgment and distort reality. Because change is a never-ending force, the only thing you can count on is that things will never go exactly as planned. So, how do you maintain consistency and alignment? You do it by beginning with the red lines of what cannot change.

Let me tell you from experience, that implementation of this concept is a lot harder than you might suspect. If there is a parental owner's manual, I've never seen one. Though I grew up in an extremely religious environment, the strict rules/social structure approach never worked for me. The parameters had the opposite effect. They made me less observant. If you have ever felt like you were living a lie, you can understand my early life. "I do not measure up" meant, "I am useless and defective."

It took me many years to find myself and come out, so to speak, as desiring to live a more modern lifestyle. Believe me when I say this language is appropriate. Facing your very observant parents and telling them you want to follow a more "secular" lifestyle produces trauma and hysteria and – more trauma and hysteria. The accompanying shame and sadness are profound and hurtful. I have even seen parents observe the rules of mourning for children who have selected a path like mine. Harsh, I know but the Gold Standard is simply that black and white for some.

You can imagine how much harm these feelings caused and how the emotional shrapnel spewed into my everyday life. Finding peace with God and religion presented both a challenge and a considerable journey that I am certainly a better person for having experienced but believe me when I tell you: the "Gold Standard Concept" can be brutal.

Going deeper, it is the very benefit of the Gold Standard that makes it so difficult. The standard's rigidity lies at the heart of why so many children from good families go astray. Somehow Frances and Hank found a way to make it work for all three. Others I know did too.

How did they manage and what can we learn from them?

In interviewing multiple parents like Frances and Hank, I was able to break the Gold Standard down into five themes:
- Accountability
  - It all begins with I. Only "I" can do it
  - No one will fight harder for me than me
- Vision
  - What do I want? What do I need?

- ○ Consider your goals carefully; don't just go with the flow
- Consistency
  - ○ Never stop trying, testing and acting
  - ○ Manage the small stuff as efficiently as possible
- Risk Management
  - ○ Know how to listen, reflect and act
  - ○ Be careful to recognize when you may be off course
- Transparency
  - ○ Never lose sight of what really matters
  - ○ Be honest in your interactions

Obviously, you can create as many subcategories as you wish or require. These are simply the common themes from my friends and family. Your "lines in the sand" may differ.

While every Transformation Initiative and every client are different, no matter the role I am asked to play, I never compromise on the five categories above. I always make sure everything we do has a clear, single owner. This is true even for tasks I assign myself; I hold myself to the same standard as I do others. Funny how you can peer pressure yourself to be better when expectations are clear.

I never forget that transformation, whether planned or unplanned, must always have clear goals. You need to know where you are headed in order to get there. Considering goals carefully is about being unafraid to dream and even dream big. Be honest with what you really want to achieve and write it down. You will be surprised about how this act alone can often define success.

I also use routines but the key is to not get locked into a single type of routine or approach. For example, as you saw earlier, the routine of frequent daily prayer never worked for me. Yet, I found equal if not better closeness and commitment to my faith by finding other approaches like meditation and community. The same is true in the corporate world where I use tools like Agile when I need them, but I similarly opt out when they seem inappropriate. In authoring this book. I used Agile techniques during editing because I was eager to get it done and done right. I did not however use Agile in the writing process because I did not want the target at the end to stifle the journey.

Balancing risk and return is a very complicated and personal idea. What may be risky to you is opportunity to me. I always wanted to jump out of a plane, but my debilitating fear of heights continues to prevent me from giving it a go. Therefore, the best change leaders always take time to listen to fears, take them seriously, and react carefully to them. Everyone knows the expression, "Where there's smoke, there's fire." The truth is, in life, sometimes there really is only smoke but that does not mean it cannot kill you. In fact, I have failed more in my life because of smoke than from the flames. Knowing how to listen and how to balance risk are key requirements for any change leader worthy of the position.

Family first is a code I live by in my professional life as well as in my personal life. Before you think hiring me will be like bringing in an organized crime syndicate, let me explain.

Times of transformation are strange and confusing. People get emotional and lost. Their fear can be debilitating and may make them do funny things like complaining to your boss, ignoring data, or completely going off the deep end. We sometimes do the same in our personal lives when a traumatic transformational event happens. "I don't know who you are anymore," is a phrase uttered in more homes than we care to imagine. I do not believe most of us, "go nuts." Instead, the emotion and stress of the moments(s) overcome us and we do not act like ourselves.

At these times, family, and our core relationships tower in their importance. If we do not trust each other and rely on our interdependence, we are on our own and vulnerable. Our camaraderie gives us strength.

I use this understanding during complicated change efforts in a variety of ways. I remain extra sensitive and strive never to contradict my team during a meeting with their boss. I may approach them afterwards and guide the conversation if it is really going off the rails, but I do it in a very thoughtful way. I take great pains to be transparent in everything I do so people see this approach in measurable deeds and actions. As people become comfortable, they follow suit and the team acts as one.

I hold everyone to the same standard – including myself.

There is nothing I hate more than when my children compete for my love. Don't roll your eyes, all kids do it. Think not? Bring only one kid a gift when you come home from a trip – write me and tell me how that went. Even when it's justified. I identify the behavior and stamp it out immediately.

In meetings, some have found me tough (at times abrasive) but one thing they never doubt is that I do my best to apply rules fairly. I will call myself out for missing a date the same way I will someone else because in a family, we are all equal. When people see this, they respond and instinctively get it.

Consider my interpretation of the Gold Standard. I build flexibility into the very things that should not be flexible, but I do it in a way that is always consistent, simple, clear, and measurable. In this way I do not break the standard but rather define it and make it manageable. This is what people crave when facing massive, scary change. The more consistent you are in the application, the more loyalty and success you will find. It's as simple as that.

Early on, like many inexperienced people, I approached management and projects with the subtlety of a battering ram. I pushed and worked as hard as I could until we completed the assigned task. Sometimes it worked – other times, not so much. But one thing never changed:

At the end of every single project, every single person hated me.

Somewhere along the way, I figured out that transformation does not operate according to a timeline. It is a response to massive stimuli. Each "interference" requires a response – carefully considered and appropriately applied. For the transformation to prove effective (for it to "stick" and be productive within a given organization), you have to balance the fact that you may walk across "the red lines" and this may become offensive.

The idea is to take the time and identify your Gold Standard as well as the Gold Standard of the key stakeholders on the team. Once you know where the no-fly zones are, you can help make others malleable. At the very least, you will know where the landmines are located.

Indeed, with this knowledge you can become more predictive about when and where there will be a flashpoint (Organization ESP again). When you get good at this, you can even use "controlled explosions" to push a change to the next level in record time. This goes for a company as well as our personal lives.

I am grateful to know people like Frances and Hank and to have had their guidance throughout my life. Even when I was unhappy and confused as a kid, their warmth and clarity of purpose always helped me know where I stood and determine what I did and did not want.

Thank you for helping me find the path home.

Key Takeaways:

- When working through times of massive change, always take the time to define "The Gold Standard" a set of solid lines that cannot be crossed no matter what
- Transformation is complicated and confusing and emotions can cloud our judgment and distort reality. By defining your no-fly zones, you have a better chance of keeping alignment and maintaining collaboration
- As you apply the Gold Standard, be sure to use consistency, interpretation and flexibility in your approach or you may break people when the going gets tough

- Consistently applying the standard is key for success during times of immense change. People crave certainty when the world around them is changing

CHAPTER 8: THE AMI PRINCIPLE

I want to close this section by relating how friendship has helped me succeed. Growing up, I never had many friends. For those who know me now, this may seem odd since we have folks over regularly and I am always doing something with other people.

When I was a kid, friends were not the norm in my house. Outside of synagogue, my mother's immediate family, and one or two acquaintances, I cannot think of any time when my parents entertained, went out with anyone, or showed much interest in anything social. My parents were (and still are) busy people who put supporting their family over having fun or making relationships outside of the home.

My life changed when I met my wife. Sara taught me how friends make life richer than any amount of money. Having friends visit for meals, going to the movies, sharing in happy occasions, or consoling each other during sad ones enriches everything about life.

It's funny, the older I get the more I realize how much people need each other. Think back to the "Fosbury Flop" story at the beginning of this book. Without the inspiration from my daughter, I would likely not be writing this work today.

Whenever I begin a transformational program, I invariably have the same conversation with the CEO.

"So, Nathan, you've been here a few weeks, tell me what you think of my people."

"Sure, I am happy to share some observations. Where would you like me to focus my comments?"

"Let's start with overall and then dig into this or that problematic person."

Even though some people find similar conversations uncomfortable, I love them. Using my psychology-based approach, I often have a very clear understanding of the company, the people and where big traps are within a matter of days. When the CEO opens the door, I can share my hypotheses. (It helps that I have a good track record.)

Given the Fearless Honesty to which I am committed, my meetings sometimes leave the CEO in a weird place. On one hand I probably confirm many suspicions – both a good and bad thing. On the other hand, the CEO must consider his/her reaction after hearing the reflections of someone who was hired "as an expert." It usually means there is a need for action. But what kind of action?

Because my observations often involve people who are hostile to the transformation or who can (or want to) impede the overarching team's ability to move forward, time is also of the essence.

If a CEO asks for my opinion on what to do first, I often refer to The Gold Standard. Resistance to a transformation must be treated seriously. A good Transformation Lead must identify those with deep seated, never transform attitudes from those who are merely afraid. Each requires its own approach or medicine and treating one the same way as the other can lead to certain doom. By going back to the Gold Standard of yourself or your organization, you can quickly identify those that are stepping out of line from those who have stepped over the line and are in another country.

Once you have established the inviolate nature of The Gold Standard, use repetition, consistency and data from delivery to drive the project forward. The kinetic energy released from the momentum will bring even the most intransigent folks on board while truly exposing those who no matter what, will never change. The former are trained and coached the latter are quickly let go. Leaders who can't do this burn needless efficiency and cost.[34]

The Gold Standard forms the basis or contract on which our relationships are based. This "relationship contracting" represents a critical foundation in any business association. The best part: we each control acceptance of the contract and the rules by which our interactions are governed.

Let's illustrate these concepts by comparing two recent Transformational Initiatives at roughly equal size organizations.

Scenario 1: Private Equity Portfolio Company. The project was to implement a new operating model as the company shifted its core go-to market strategy. The CEO was overly concerned about interpersonal relationships and this unfortunately resulted in an inability to govern his team. At the start of the initiative it became clear that one of the most important stakeholders, the head of operations, was having difficulty with the new approach. She often used language like, "I don't understand the approach" and, "I have no capacity to do any of this." Still, the project was a smashing success. The turning point came after three months, when I shared data from our newly created operational reporting. The data revealed it was neither her capacity nor an inability to understand that was causing this leader to fail.

The data simply did not support her arguments and everyone around her began to realize it.

After a few weeks of trying to appease her, the data made it obvious that it was her attitude that was the real problem. In fact, I had real data demonstrating how her poor outlook caused an efficiency loss of ~$5-$10 million annually. Anytime she was asked to do anything, she complained, ruined meetings, and distracted the team. Once, I tracked as she wasted hours of multiple team members' time on a non-issue that was solved with a fifteen-minute conversation. Multiply this by 1,000 and you can see the scope of the disaster. Whenever you see a once great

Fortune 500 with all the money in the world topple over due to its operations, in my experience, this is the most common cause.

To his credit, when the CEO was presented with this data he acted. He met with the leader and began by reinforcing the core goals of the effort which she clearly agreed with. The CEO then helped her understand he was committed to her and got her executive coaching. This leader is now the Chief Operating Officer and a key contributor to a very fast-growing firm in a new market.

Scenario 2: Global transformation in a large division of a leading financial services firm. The CEO was very strong and demanded that all her leadership team sign their names to a board to show their support for the program. The new leadership team of high-powered executives chaffed a little. Begrudgingly, they all signed. The project was very complicated with the future of the division and a nine-figure investment at stake. Throughout the project, key C-Suite executives caused challenges. From badmouthing the process, to catapulting team members in open meetings, these folks were hard-nosed, and it showed.

Upon presentation of the data, the CEO sat the real trouble maker down. She told him how this Transformation represented the future of the company and if he was not on-board he should resign now. The Leader opted to stay and the CEO said he was glad. The CEO closed the meeting by pulling out a photograph he had taken of the board with the signatures on it. He said:

"Remember, your commitment is more than words."

After this meeting the Leader continued to obstruct, though passively and in a more deceitful way. After a few months it got back to the CEO that this leader had begun questioning the leadership and direction of the division, not just the wisdom of the program. This leader was then "managed out" or fired over the course of a few months by diminishing his role, slowly at first and then cutting it off in one fell swoop.

The program was ultimately a massive success and resulted in a new front-to-back operating model including a new technology infrastructure and digital ecosystem.

These projects could not have been more different. The only commonality they shared was the difficult leaders – "obstructers" in some circles. Whatever you call them, you get the idea. They occupy key roles in the organization. As a result, they can "flat a tire" in any project. Their engagement and support are critical.

So, how did I succeed?

The answer, of course, lies with understanding the individuals involved. As I got to know the leader in Scenario 1 it was clear she agreed with the Gold Standard. She knew this project was fundamental for the organization's future and really wanted it to succeed. As you can infer from her wording, "she" felt that she could not do the work on time and to her standard. She did not disagree with the program; she did not trust herself.

This assessment was reinforced by her own people. As I got deeper with the team everyone had this or that story about how this leader had helped them over a weekend during a time of extreme stress. This leader was just a good person who didn't know what to do and was afraid and simply speaking irrationally because of the transformation.

When I presented the data through this lens, the CEO immediately got it and tailored his approach accordingly.

In Scenario 2 it became obvious the difficult leader in question did not agree with the Gold Standard. Whenever I asked him whether he agreed with the basics, he had story after story about why the effort and ultimately the company would fail. Sometimes they tried it before and others, they were simply "not smart enough as an organization to possibly execute. So, why try?"

As my career moves on, I am always surprised about how frequently this attitude appears. Sadly, it can often not be fixed because both sides have simply had enough and no longer want to try. In this case, again from the wording, you note the focus on everyone not being good. This person fundamentally did not believe in the organization and my project was just another opportunity to vent his misalignment.

These individuals require the harsh approach the CEO in this story took. To quote one of my favorite movies, *The Lady-killers*, "I smite, you smite, he smites, we done smote!" Translation: "To smite means to go upside the head. Because sometimes brothers and sisters, it's the only way."[35]

Implementing the Gold Standard consistently over the course of months, in each case we engaged in consistent forums governed by consistent rules. We each held the other to the Standard, which led to positive results and happier people along the way.

It took me years but I realize now that relationships, are not binary. Change evokes fear. Sometimes, even the most flexible rules of the Gold Standard are violated and by extension so is the relationship. This is a very confusing thing for Transformation Leads. On one hand you want to call someone out, escalate the situation to their boss, and scream, "Breach of contract!" On the other hand, cooler heads want the conflict avoided.

That's why overcoming these challenges begins with aligning around the Gold Standard. You need to set clear rules to form the basis of trust and mutual respect. However, it is ultimately in the execution that the change comes to life.

As you have probably seen by now, this is where the force of Consistency can be used effectively. Consistency comes in many forms. From having meetings at a set time with a set agenda to eating at the same time daily. Consistent ritual is the best way to ingrain a habit, but the idea only works when you agree to put it into practice.

As the transformation is governed by consistent rules, the Transformation Lead creates predictability and norms that all can understand. As I mentioned earlier, repetition is often the best defense to change's never-ending assault. The more ingrained the rules the more obvious the appropriate reaction. When you see life this way you begin to realize that people are rarely jerks (if ever). They are often just scared. Once you know where people lie, it becomes fairly simple to manage the situation and drive the change.

Before we close this chapter, I do want to share some thoughts on empathy and how important this is when applying the Gold Standard.

You will always hear some stupid comment like, "It's not personal – it's only business." Well, if a project is going to ruin someone's job, *it is always personal.* When a leader remembers the delicate nature of every shift and maneuver from a "people point of view," stellar results often follow.

Earlier I mentioned Fosbury Incorporated – my first client. When I began with them, I encountered a significant problem: I did not have any money. I could not afford the legal work I needed to begin. Desperate, I called my good friend – Ami – a corporate lawyer, for help and advice.

My buddy never failed me. He always took my calls even when he was in his car and grinding his way home after another long day. He advised me on negotiations to contracts and everything in between. I can honestly say, my company, Simpel and Associates, would not be around today without Ami and I am eternally grateful for what he did for me in the spirit of friendship.

But the relationship was not one-sided. We had become friends a few years earlier. We shared a mutual love of family, nature, and the great outdoors. Our children spent magical summer days together. We enjoyed joyous occasions and endured sad ones. Ami and I were always there for each other. When I needed some help, he understood the intensely personal nature of my need. He knew me – he wanted me to succeed.

Business relationships work better when leaders take the time to appreciate how personal work is to those they manage and lead. The more engaged you are as a leader, the more inherently your colleagues will want to assist you in the quest for success and excellence.

Empathy does not take a fancy business degree. You don't

have to hire a consultant. All it takes is the interest – and the time – to try to "occupy someone else's space." When "Eddie in Accounting" is in a bad mood – when "Irene in Logistics" makes a nasty comment – what's going on? Everyone gets angry – everyone loses it from time to time. But what's driving the reaction?

A personal issue? A health crisis? Is it possible *you* screwed up or failed to explain something adequately?

Sure, "time is money," but taking the time to inquire, appreciate, sympathize, and listen to those around you will result in massive productivity and achievement. Those are in addition to being just a decent human being.

In every project, look for the "worker bees," the men and women who bust it behind the scenes to get things done. They are not always good at self-promotion – they fly under the radar. Many of them come across as annoying because they dot all the i's and cross all the t's.[36] Most of the time, they are not looking for fame; they just want things done right.

Saying "thank you" goes a long way. Do it in public – do it in private if you think they might otherwise be embarrassed. Your expression of gratitude only takes a second or two, but these key doers will respond to your kindness with enthusiasm.

Simple, yes. Common sense, yes. But not as prevalent as you may think.

Empathy (and courtesy) can diffuse difficult and naturally tense situations so common to Transformational Initiatives. And you will be surprised about how infectious they can be. Simple acts of kindness and putting yourself in other peoples' positions can help to generate a gracious atmosphere of positive cooperation.

One of my favorite movies is the '80s cult classic *Bill and Ted's Excellent Adventure.*[37] It has a great line: "Be excellent to each other..." No, not exactly Shakespeare but the phrase sums up what good relationship management is all about.

What is the Ami principle?

Treating people with respect will lead to strictly greater

results than not.

Oh yeah... and...

"Party on, dudes!"[38]

Key Takeaways:

• Use the Gold Standard to distinguish between noise and a real problem. When you identify the real problems, have the courage to act
• Repetition is often the best defense to change's never-ending assault. The more in grained the rules the more obvious the outliers and appropriate reaction
• Take the time to build empathy. Relationships are some of the best tools for winning at change. Empathy only takes a second and can go a long way
• Treating people with respect will lead to strictly greater results than not

Section 3: Society

When I was five, we only had access to four channels and commercials comprised an annoying but unavoidable reality in the television watching experience.

One day, my cartoon world was interrupted by a very weird ad. The spot showed three guys dressed in cool jackets who danced '80s style and sang about registering for something called "Selective Service."

Out of nowhere, the trio of dancing fools grabbed some random guy at a bus stop and accompanied him to the Post Office where he signed a form.

In an instant, the man is transformed.

With his own bodacious, shiny jacket, he too was now part of the club.

The voiceover explained, "When you turn eighteen, go to the Post Office to register for Selective Service." The spot ended with all four guys giving four thumbs way the hell up.

Sheesh!

Curious as ever, I asked my mother about the commercial. She explained that the public service announcement was about registering for the draft into the U.S. Army.

Over the next few days, I saw the commercial several more times and began to understand that "signing up" was – as the spot said – "the Law."

Upon reflection my infantile mind was severely troubled. Would I have to leave my home? Would I have to fight in a war. Would I live to be nineteen?

I could not get the dread of charging into battle (and being shot) out of my mind.

One night, my parents rushed into my room when they heard me as I sobbed. When they discovered the source of my distress, my mother stroked my hair while my father explained how the draft was no longer active. Even though I still had to register,[39] I would only have to serve in the Armed Forces if I wanted to.

In retrospect, the event was more humorous than traumatic. (The commercial has not aged well.[40]) But, it is obvious that the people who put the commercial on the air (intending to ramp up the Selective Service numbers) did not assume that their target audience would be watching *The* Smurfs or *Inspector Gadget*. While they missed their demographic, the spot made a deep impression on a little kid from the Bronx New York.

During times of change, people can sometimes react the same way I did to the commercial. Every sense stands on high alert – emotions are raw, at best.

Research shows that losing a job has a profound impact on mental health and believe me when I tell you this is true.[41]

With so much sensitivity around, how should a change leader approach communication during times of Transformation?

With so much uncertainty, every letter of every word of every communication is parsed as people look for deeper meaning into their fate and what will happen next.

If you say nothing you missed the boat. If you unintentionally use the wrong wording you can wreak havoc like driving up anxiety. So, what's a leader to do?

As I sit here and thump on the keys, the world crumbles in the face of the COVID-19 outbreak. Everyone wants to blame – ah – anyone else: the President, the former President, the Chinese, immigrants, people wearing masks, people not wearing masks, Dr. Fauci, bats. Every time someone gives a new "definitive answer," someone else rebuts the point within minutes. We are aiming a pea shooter and trying to hit a saucer-sized target from 200 yards away in a blustering crosswind.

While the Transformational Initiatives I deal with are, of course, less scary than a global pandemic, they carry their own threat levels. If you've ever experienced such a program, you've heard the questions at the water cooler: "How many people are they cutting?" "What about that idiot in Accounting?" "Is my job safe?"

There are more, most of which are internal: "How will I

balance making my clients happy while delivering the change work?" "This stupid new idea is work; why should I bother?" As a Transformational Lead who has been doing this for more than twenty years, I have seen and heard it all. I even once watched a frustrated analyst rush out of a room screaming only to slam the door on her leg.

Stress sure makes you do funny things.

Media and communications represent primary tools for the Transformation Lead. In the right hands, they can provide comfort and offer a rallying point. Improperly utilized, they can increase the chaos and crash the entire project.

I don't have all the answers about communication and a full discussion is well outside the scope of this book (maybe a sequel?). However, in the interest of providing some guidance, I am going to take a somewhat fun approach to this topic.

If movies, music, and media influenced me so much, perhaps there are tidbits we can glean from some of my favorites about how to communicate during transformations.

The following section contains details of some of the most influential pieces of media I have encountered and how they changed my thinking. I hope you can use the ideas to develop a greater sensitivity for the power of media and communication during times of change and to begin to understand how to create meaningful connections with an audience.

If not, hey it will still be fun, I promise.

Key Takeaways:

• Times of immense change can cause people to act wildly out of character. Always remember this and be sensitive as you build relationships and interact with others
• Media and communications represent pri mary tools for the Transformation Lead to drive outcomes. In the right hands, they can provide comfort and offer a rallying point. Improperly

utilized, they can increase the chaos and crash
the effort

CHAPTER 9: LESSONS FROM ANCIENT SCOTLAND

It was a lovely late winter Saturday and I was having lunch with my wife and middle child. My son had just completed another week at his new middle school and was telling us about his latest accomplishments.

Turns out, Isaac, an avid amateur businessman, had begun a new elective class: Intro to Business. Like his old man, my son enjoys understanding how business and commerce work; the new class was right up his alley.

The class had been learning about leadership and Isaac wanted to know how I recognize a good leader. I thought about his question and, wanting to give him one of my typical, out-of-the-box answers, said, "What do you think? Who do you think is a good leader?"

To my delight, he responded, "Braveheart."

Braveheart,[42] he explained, typified a leader because he led his people through the horrors of war and helped them realize their dream of independence.

Great answer, I thought, but I wanted him to go deeper.

"So, then, a good leader is someone who delivers results? But results, are the outcome and do not tell you how you got there. How does a leader deliver on these outcomes?"

We dissected questions like this for a bit and ultimately landed at three ways to know whether you have a good leader –

someone who:

- Delivers a core message
- Inspires people to work towards that message
- Has people who stand for him/her

Throughout the film we see the power of a great leader to inspire and drive people forward using a clear and unambiguous message. Take the idea of family. One of the most touching, underappreciated aspects of Braveheart is the relationship between two of Wallace's key lieutenants; his friend, Hamish,[43] and his father, Campbell,[44] or, as I call him, "The Old Man." Each character portrayed heroism, courage, and dedication.

I'm not sure you'd want either man as a character reference on your resume, but they are pretty badass. I mean, some dude cuts Campbell's hand off during the Battle of Stirling. The old man never blinks before he kills the guy. When he's shot with an arrow, the Old Man still lifts a gate over his head, so the townspeople can rush into the inner courtyard and end the skirmish. Hamish is a wild man throughout the film.

To me, the most endearing part of these characters comes in how they relate to each other. Nowhere else is there a better example than in their last scene.

Campbell: I'm dying. Let me be.
Hamish: No. You're going to live.
Campbell: I've lived long enough to live free. And proud to see you become the man that you are. I'm a happy man.

They never say it, but the message is clear. The men are on the same page; their lives are summarized in three words: family, loyalty, love. There are no grand speeches – no declarations of eternal affection. They have spoken through their actions and their dedication to one another – a key aspect to effective and lasting communication.

The same can be said of great leaders. Sure, they have outstanding teams, but the leader puts the team together – attracts, inspires, and brings out the best in each member. The best leaders accomplish this because they stand for something simple and approachable.

For example, let's a play a little game. Think of a great leader and think of a word to describe him or her and you will quickly see what I mean.

Michael Jordan = competitor

Warren Buffet = value

Golda Meir = decisive

Steve Jobs = innovator

Like all things, when you understand the world at its core, it becomes quite easy to identify the good ones (those with a clear, easily identifiable message) from those who are poor leaders.

Looking at leadership this way also gives leaders more power to refocus and even reinvent themselves.

Like take Bill Gates. Early in his career, many would have likely called him a bully. A genius, sure, but also a very tough, take no prisoners type of fighter.

Now if you ask someone about Bill Gates they would likely say "humanitarian."

Sure, it took Mr. Gates years and billions of dollars to change his core message and get the public to believe it but that's why he's Bill Gates. For the average person, it is simpler, of course, but you get the idea. Once you identify your simple core message, you can create focused plans to change it and that's a good thing.

Leaders also make sure that their core message is inspiring.

There is a common conversation within academic circles about the difference between a manager and a leader. To me, the ability to have this easy to identify core message and for it to be inspiring are core differences. A leader inspires people to go above and beyond even what they think they can. Another key contributor to **Transformation Arbitrage**.[45]

While shrouded by the mists of history, within the context of the movie, William Wallace unquestionably embodied the key attributes of community and family. Most importantly, he communicated a single, inspiring core message:

F-rrrrrrrrrr-eeeee-dom!

This message, combined with his actions inspired people who were starving and outnumbered to beat a far superior enemy. Now that's over and above results!

Leading organizations recognize the importance of a core message and work closely with HR Departments to attract people who will buy in and support it.

When I assess management talent, I scrutinize an individual's ability to convey a program's core message. What I see tells me a lot about the likelihood of a leader's chances to be successful within the organization. If the individual is not aligned at the core, everything will become a lot more difficult; even basic communication.[46] This can cost companies a lot more than you think.

For example, I once did some work with a well-known local charity. It was experiencing trouble – a lot of things to fix. Despite hovering on the verge of insolvency (and barely making payroll), there were people who worked 60-70-hour work weeks for the cause.

Immediately I saw very clear ways to help increase efficiency and to extend their budget's reach – simple things like not running community programs for one person and automating the phone answering processes.

Whenever I elevated my ideas to the Executive Director, I heard the classic resister lines: "We do that already." Or "we've already tried that." No matter what I said, the organization ignored my advice. Ultimately, I departed.

In retrospect, I should have realized that not-for-profits are unique entities. Sometimes they really are "not for profit" and are just good people wanting to do good things. Business reasoning, no matter how grounded in data, will never trump their passion and that's wonderful. Even though the data was telling me the place was a disaster and aesthetically unpleasing, the charity had volunteers with over twenty years of experience putting in three times the effort of well-paid Fortune 500 employees.

Anomaly? Maybe.

But the situation illustrates the power of a message.

I should have saved myself a lot of time and just written a check. Hardcore capitalists think differently, and I simply do not have enough experience in the not-for-profit space. I missed the core message. When I hear protectionist arguments not rooted in data, I respond in terms of "efficiency" and "practicability." What I really want to say is, "This suggestion will make things better. Just do it, damn it!"

But what I have learned from interpreting their core message is efficiency and practicality often do not matter. The real issue? What if (because of my cuts): "Someone doesn't not get the services they need?" I am not wise enough to answer that question and I will never try again until I am ready to commit the time to learn the correct situational approach.

When people are aligned to a core message and are inspired by it, they will go above and beyond. Even if all business logic tells them otherwise.

Great leaders rally people to stand for them, so they do not have to stand for themselves. Real leaders don't need or demand recognition. It follows them because the people with whom they work will shout the accomplishments from the rooftops without any prompting.

Following their first major battle in *Braveheart*, the Scots assemble before the Council to receive medals and accolades. The Head of the Council tells William Wallace to "stand and be recognized."

I love the scene, not so much for the pomp and circumstance but for the great simplicity of the line. Wallace accepts recognition with reluctance and finds the first opportunity to leave the hall with his generals. He does not say anything; his men follow instinctively because, despite the great toll in effort, blood, and lives, the team recognizes the bloody work must continue. The "English will be back" and rather than fight for scraps, Wallace and crew understand the mission and will not be distracted from its pursuit: Frrrrrrreeeedom!

One of my favorite ideas from the Agile methodology is that of team empowerment. The team is smart enough to make its own decisions in the day to day. In fact, empowering the team properly enables faster and more meaningful outcomes because you don't have to wait to organize, educate, and sell a decision to people (often leaders) who are many times removed from the trenches.

When great leaders deliver an inspirational core message, the team will come together to deliver outcomes and the members will remain connected and know instinctively what to do next. Imagine being a Fortune 500 company with a work force that all understand what needs to be done – and can do it – without being told. You would be successful beyond your wildest dreams and with much less stress. This translates into happier employees who support or stand for the message. This support for the CEO's implementation of the vision is what you see in every top organization.

The best leaders maintain a dynamic feeling even in the worst of times.

For example, client's often ask me how I maintain momentum on projects that may result in detrimental impacts to the very workers on the project. (Sometimes outsourcing a department requires effort from the people who will likely be displaced. How do I keep them motivated?)

For now, let's simplify the answer: empathy, compensation, and honesty to be sure. But continuing engagement also requires honesty and alignment on the reason. If people understand what they are doing and believe it is the right thing for the company (or that the project makes sense), you will find a higher degree of collaboration and success even when the worst happens.

And guess what? It will ultimately cost you *a lot less* while putting the workers in a better spot for their next role. The workers stand on their own for the leader and her vision even when it scares them, because they believe.

Now that's leadership.

As my son and I agreed on the positive lessons of leadership promoted in *Braveheart* I could not help but be proud. It was great to share something with my son that had spoken with such eloquence to me as a kid. It's funny, but as we mature, symbols (as presented by art, music, and drama) mean more to us, especially when we can share them with someone we love.

Key Takeaways:

- During times of change, leadership is more important than ever. This person(s) provides direction and maintains motivation throughout the initiative
- A great leader is someone who
  - o Delivers a core message
  - o Inspires people
  - o Has people who stand for him/her
- Once you identify your simple core message, you can create focused plans to change it
- When people are aligned to a core message and are inspired by it, they will go above and beyond. Even if all business logic tells them other wise
- If people understand what they are doing and believe it is right There will be a higher degree of collaboration and success

CHAPTER 10:
THE GENIUS

I will never forget the first time I heard music as a sentient person capable of thinking and understanding. It was in my family's old apartment in the Bronx. The memory remains splotchy and raw, so I am guessing I was three or four. My mother put on a record of children's music by the "Mr. Rogers of the Jewish World," Uncle Moishy.[47]

It's crazy to consider, but my wife who was born in South Africa heard the very same songs and we introduced them to our kids over twenty years later. Uncle Moishy was viral before it was a thing.

As I grew up, my tastes in music changed. I devoured everything: religious music, classical music, all the way to one of my favorites of all time, Queen.[48] In fact, the first non-religious CD I ever bought was *Classic Queen* in 1992 after my father broke the rules and bought me my first Discman.

One day in my late thirties, I realized I hadn't done much music listening in years. I could not recall the last album I bought or the last time I spent an hour replaying a song again and again in search of each distinguishing nuance. I didn't even have good headphones. What had happened? I guess I was so busy building a life that I just lost track of something I once thought important.

How sad.

I decided to act, which led me to discover EDM[49] and Avicii and well, if you've gotten this far, you know the rest...

Many of my closest friends have asked me why I am so obsessed? I mean Zeppelin, okay, but Avicii?

Well...

Avicii delivers beautiful, melodic, emotion. From the rhythmic bump of *Wake Me Up* to the angst in *Hey Brother.* The album, *True,* is an EDM classic.

His next album, *Stories,* sees use of even more genres. But no matter the genre, all of *Avicii's* music is melodic, fun and leaves you feeling a wide range of emotions.

But what really made Avicii a genius was his ability to combine his music with videos where he wove intricate stories that brought the music to life in unique ways. For example:

- *Levels:* Man is a "circle" living in a world of "square." Although he tries to hide the truth, the effort is like pushing a bolder up a mountain.[50] But, his spirit perseveres and breaks free, infecting others with the groove and saving mankind. One of the best videos ever made, period.
- *Pure* Grinding: The sign on the movie theater early in the video, is the first indication that Avicii connects the theme of his albums True and Stories by delivering videos that are in fact true stories of the people around him or that he dreams up. It's also a cool gangster story, so check it out.
- *Broken Arrows*: I've already mentioned this one. Changed my life.

I could go on for hours, but you get the idea. Avicii combined sound and visual mediums with mastery.[51]

His brilliance crosses genres as well. *Levels* has a Picasso-esque feel; *Hey Brother* leans on bluegrass roots. Avicii effortlessly captures different emotions and styles. The first time I saw the video for *Hey Brother*, I could not believe how perfectly a Swedish native captured the American ideals of patriotism, duty, and family.

One video that jolted me, *I Could Be the One,* tells the story of a woman I like to call "Truth." Every day, she wakes up to the same routine: annoying alarm, brushing teeth, and going to a job where she is surrounded by shallow social cliques. Truth's interactions are awkward and often unkind ("Maybe you should just have my salad instead"), with no room for acceptance or understanding.

When Truth closes her eyes at night, she dreams of being free from the constraints of the real world. On her island, she is queen and does what she wants with whom she wants. Quite liberating indeed.

The story jump cuts or flashes sideways (thank you, *Lost*[52]) between her sad life and dream world until they can no longer coexist. Unable to resist her identity, Truth explodes – the real person inside bursts forth with the only acceptable answer: she must break free.[53]

Truth finally escapes the prison of her mind, and she races towards her dreams, now within her reach. She bursts out of her building's back door; you hear her solidify her "goals" by booking, "One- way, Barbados." On the way to her parking spot, she clicks open her office door, steps off the curb to cross the street, and...

Splat – she's killed by a van displaying the word "Rush" on the side.

Freaking brilliant.

The very same fateful night I first saw *Broken Arrows*, I watched *I Could be the One* for the first time and set to work on Simpel and Associates. When you think about life and change, only one thing is certain: shit...always...happens. There is no such thing as risk free or truly safe. We are all in a world of random occurrence where perfectly healthy, righteous people like my mother-in-law develop a tumor and die in six months at the age of sixty while the a-hole guy down the street who smokes three packs of cigarettes a day lives to be 100.

It took me forty-plus years to understand how the random nature of life might contribute to anxiety. How can anyone live without fear when anything can happen at any time? I rank caring for my family above all else. What if I fail them?

There are just so many possibilities; how could I ever plan for all of them? To make matters worse, for anyone not named Gates or Buffett, who thinks they have enough money? When what I am not anticipating happens, will I (or those I leave behind) have enough?

Feels a little frantic, doesn't it? Well – duh! Debilitating anxiety affects and afflicts millions. The situation will only escalate as society continues to accelerate. We will see more – and younger – sufferers. If we do not create more awareness and understanding on how to manage the issue better, we will face an insurmountable problem.[54]

With so many challenges in the world, how does one manage anxiety?

In working with companies, professionals and myself, I have found that the answer begins with understanding change. As I described earlier, you must first accept that change, and by extension risk, is real and unending. You must also recognize that you have tools, no matter who you are or what you have been through, to fight back (remember, we are all artists). Then you must learn to work with the change by focusing on your goals and what you know. With consistent messaging and action you will quickly see results which will give you confidence and momentum (kinetic energy) to see it through.

By approaching risk with this frame of mind, you avoid making frantic, anxiety driven decisions. You start to think about things differently and with a little practice it becomes second nature.

The best change leaders do this effectively by building risk management into the very culture of their organization. They know how to use messaging and consistent action to create alignment, inspire action and use the power of a team to make it through even the most challenging times.

This is especially true when there are macro level forces you cannot control but can impact you substantially on a personal level.

Perhaps the best example of such a scenario was my experience after 9-11.

It was early in my career and I was working for a leading financial services company.

I remember everything about that day.

I recall vividly being greeted by the smell of smoke and the sight of charred presentations blowing in the wind when I emerged from the subway.

My legs still ache when I think about what it felt like to run for my life when the first tower fell.

I also remember how I thought it was so ironic that the smoke from the tower made it look like a blizzard even though the day had started out warm and sunny.

I still get chills when I think about making it to the Brooklyn Bridge and looking out at beautiful downtown only to see the second tower explode and crumble into dust.

And I still feel relief when I think about how unlike many others, I did finally make it home. I remember how I cried when I saw my wife and daughter after thinking only a few hours earlier that it would never happen again.

Yes, it was a harrowing day and there's a lot more to tell (see my talk "what I learned from 9-11"). For now what I do want to mention is how the company I worked for responded.

While 9-11 was a major national calamity and of course I expected a response, what I did not expect was how empathetic that response would be. It began with management's unwavering, unified statements about safety first. This was quickly followed by supporting actions like giving the entire New York staff a month off as the rubble smoldered.

As the weeks unfolded, the clear message of "safey, action and then business" was reinforced through frequent global town halls with the CEO and regular sessions with division leadership. These sessions were followed by even more supporting action like when the company went so far as to set up an acute grief counselor network at the company's expense.

The response was so thorough and the messaging so consistent, everyone quickly fell into line. From team leads to individual contributors we all began to speak the same way about "our response" and felt empowered to act on it.

And you know what? In spite of the company's personal pain (100+ employees died in the crashes) and the ensuing global turmoil, no one lost their job. The organization emerged far stronger and remains a global leader even to this day. Now that's leadership!

I can tell you from personal experience, had leadership not reacted so fluidly to this event, things could have spiraled out of control. The anxiety could have easily overwhelmed us and prevented us from resuming business as usual for a very long time. And yet, it was simple, consistent messaging, followed by direct action that made all the difference.

The same holds true on a more localized level.

When I lead large scale change programs, anxiety can quickly become a seious problem. From the Executive VP who just bought a Jag to the line worker who wonders if the joke he told his supervisor was inappropriate, everyone begins to worry. These feeling can start under the surface and quickly become a visible brush fire that derail even the best laid plans. To put my own spin on a well-known phrase, "It's the anxiety, stupid"[55] and those who do not manage it do so at their own risk.

As you begin to work through your own personal or professional change, anxiety can and will likely emerge. If you find that it is becoming overwhelming here are some additional suggestions:

- Get the facts; act based on data
- Believe that it will all work out
- Don't be afraid to ask for help

Like I tell my kids, without facts, worrying is just a waste of energy. Figure out why you are worried then make a plan. Worrying is just trying to jog in quicksand.

Some organizations are getting better at this while others still struggle. I have seen large organizations, even as recently as a few months ago, without any regular operational reporting. If you don't know what the problem is or how big it is how can you ever hope to solve it?

While generating data is central to any successful transformation, there is also a dark side, what is routinely referred to as "analysis paralysis." It always feels good to be sure but a truckload of data can quickly overwhelm and actually create more problems. Too much data can create too many variables or make the decision bigger than it really is. You get lost in analysis and by not acting, lose the opportunity or make the decision worse.

The same is true in personal life. You see a funny looking "something" on your hand. Your first move to go to the internet, then loved ones, and then friends who live next door to doctors. Your last step (often months later) is to visit a physician's office.

Hopefully, nothing is wrong. But if you had a problem on Day 1, now – Day 235 – if something is amiss, you have wasted a lot of treatment time.

Knowing when to say "when" on data and analysis takes practice but it is a skill worth investing in.

I began developing this skill in law school when I asked my legal writing professor how he knew when he had done enough research when writting a brief. His answer: "When you start seeing the same citations and logic, you know you've got it."

The same is true here. When the pattern seems to be repeating, you generally know you've done enough leg work to make a hypothesis and act.

Data is everywhere. It just requires a mechanism to capture it. When data is used as part of communications you create a greater feeling of certainty and alignment that can help stem anxiety and push the changing organization to a more common footing.

Unfortunately, the belief part is something I cannot advise you on. Belief is personal and extremely difficult for many like me. All I can tell you is sometimes you have to just let go and trust that things will, in fact, work out. Statistics say so and experience proves it. Hopefully after reading this book you will have a new focus, approach, or appreciation for how easy it can be to take control once you just clear out the noise, see what's right in front of you, and focus on the big stuff. And hey, if you still find it hard to take the leap remember, without change there is no growth. Sometimes you must accept fate and try because if you don't, you will regret it.

If I hadn't gotten over my shyness, I wouldn't be writing a book – I would not have shared a great story about how I knew who my mother-in-law was before she even knew my name. And the same can happen for you but only if you act.

With that said, a word of caution. I have unfortunately seen what happens when anxiety spins out of control. If you do feel that things are becoming too much to handle, don't wait. Get help from a professional. Anxiety is real and can be very dangerous. There are good people out there so don't be afraid to ask.

Sadly, like so many before him, Avicii joined the 27 Club.[56]

On a personal level, I wish his family only comfort and the best.

I also want to thank Avicii for his music and for doing something magical that has so profoundly touched my life and so many others.

Peace always. Somewhere in Stockholm...

Key Takeaways:

- Anxiety affects millions of people and will only get worse as society continues to accelerate
- Anxiety also manifests itself at the organiza tion level, especially during times of extreme change. It is often overlooked and improperly managed and can be a severe impediment to transformation success
- Managing organization anxiety begins with

the right frame of mind at the top. Transformation leads set the tone with proactive communi
cation that is empathetic and supportive

• Transformation leads must also prepare for
organization anxiety during transformation programs by building in frameworks to spot it early
and manage it in a unified manner

• There is no silver bullet for defeating anxiety
but change leaders can help others work with it
by:

        o Getting the facts and

        o Inspiring belief

• Don't be afraid to ask for help. **Anxiety is real,
and can be very dangerous. If you feel it is spin-
ning out of control, do not wait. Seek help from a
professional. It may be the best decision you
ever make**

CHAPTER 11:
THE APPLESAUCE
DILEMMA

Many of you will look at the above picture and wonder what I could have possibly learned from applesauce? Let me tell you, the product depicted above had a profound influence on the way I look at marketing, branding, and product pricing.

One of my earliest jobs out of business school was for a focus group company. The company, owned and operated by the sweetest business couple I have ever met, ran two focus group facilities. They were (are) brilliant people from a long line of brilliant people. They also ran a proud, woman-owned business long before it was cool. I was excited about the prospect of helping to build a consultancy and expand it.

Over my months in the job, I had the opportunity to work on all manner of projects. Using market research, I helped create the North America go-to market strategy for one of the most highly awarded barbecue sauces in the country. Imagine spending weeks listening to people talk about their love of barbecue, how it differed from grilling, and so forth. I learned so much. For example, did you know that unlike some of the highest selling sauces, the top-rated barbecue sauces begin with a tomato-based product like tomato sauce or paste? The concoction will not burn as easily when applied to the meat. With a higher rated sauce, you can baste or cook the meat for a longer period, get more flavor, and avoid the charred texture associated with bad barbeque.

Here's another cool experience. Did you know that balsamic vinegars age like a fine wine? I'm not a big vinegar fan (weird smell and flavor) but imagine what a ten-year-aged vinegar might taste like?

We did a quick gig to help one of the leading producers of balsamic vinegar who wanted to expand in the U.S. market. When our new friends from Modena arrived, they came bearing gifts including a 30-year bottle from their personal stash.

When opened, the little flask could stink up a room in no time flat, but my boss sure seemed to love it. She kept it in the fridge with a big "hands off" sign affixed to it. I was happy to comply, but it was still cool.

Anyway, one of the products we were asked to research was a new "smoothie" company out of France. "Franz" felt he had an amazing product that was far superior to anything we had in the States. He figured with the right branding he would take the market by storm.

When the owner unveiled his masterpiece, we were all instantly impressed by... the packaging? None of us had ever seen anything like this before and could not help from commenting about it. The owner smiled and told us he had gotten his packaging from a vendor who copied it from what astronauts used. Then he encouraged us to try his smoothie.

Upon twisting the product open and taking a slurp, all the consultants had the same reaction: "This is applesauce!" The owner smiled and explained. In his country, they processed applesauce differently. It was much smoother than what we had in the States. I humbly disagreed. What ensued was one of the silliest debates of my career.

As we discussed the pluses and minuses of the product, the owner said something startling. He believed if we could position the product as a "smoothie," it would allow him to demand a much higher price point.

No one is that stupid, I thought. But, hey, we live in a world where people will pay exorbitant amounts for a shirt with a certain label. Why not try it with the smoothie?

As the focus group sessions commenced, it was clear the owner was onto something. Before offering respondents the opportunity to taste the product, we explored names and descriptions. Wouldn't you know it, the word "smoothie" had the exact effect the owner sought. When we described the product as a smoothie, respondents were far more likely to try the product. You could feel the excitement in the room when respondents had the chance to try an innovative new smoothie versus an innovative new applesauce.

One of the best moments in the project came when we discussed pricing. Our respondents were clearly our market: younger parents who would most likely buy the product and were accustomed to buying similar products in the market. I was shocked when folks suggested price points around five to eight dollars for a single pouch.

I am not sure if our applesauce friend ever launched the product in the U.S. or if he is still in business. I can't remember the name of the company at this point, but I am sure I have never seen it in all my applesauce buying years. My guess is the product either never launched or never expanded beyond a test market because once you tried it, people generally had the same reaction: "Wait, this is applesauce. No way I'm paying more than a buck – if that much."

Either way, this early event in my career really put into perspective the impact that media and pop culture can have. My time with the Smoothie Guy taught me how words can be used effectively to tie into both an emotion and dollars and cents. Indeed, good messaging can have an amplifier effect many times what you think.

I use the power of words when I communicate deliverables. Whenever I lead a program, I always take great pains to ensure all of my artifacts or work products look the same and are as simple as possible.[57] So, when someone sees something that looks like a duck, they know it will quack. More specifically, when they see my product, they know it will align to the program's core message. If you are less familiar, this is what brand management experts describe as managing and building on the core messages of a brand.

That's why I always advise my clients to take the time to define the transformational language of their program. This means identifying key terms and words that are off limits or crucial to an effort. An hour's investment up front can pay off in many millions down the line in saved hours. Miscommunication brings on over work, rework, and overall inefficiency. You want two words of advice guaranteed to help your venture soar. Here they are...

...*words matter.*

Key Takeaways:

- Some tips for effective communication during times of change:
    - o Words matter. Use them carefully
    - o Define your language up front
    - o Communicate with consistency

CHAPTER 12: YOU CAN'T EXERCISE YOUR WAY OUT OF A BAD DIET

A couple of months ago, I was in Boston visiting my father-in-law and thinking about writing this book. We had just finished taking a walk when I saw the above bicycle in the distance.

My eyesight is not what it used to be but still, even from afar, I could see there was something funky going on. The closer I got, the more unusual the contraption appeared. Always having an interest in unusual occurrences, I snapped the photograph you see above.

I studied the bike and I noticed it was basically the same thing as the Citi Bike[58] anyone in Manhattan is accustomed to seeing. While I hate giving Boston credit for anything, this bike was cooler than the Citi Bike. It featured an energy pack – more like a moped.[59] I think the idea was to cut down on emissions and traffic by using a bicycle-type solution to move commuters farther, faster. Very cool indeed.

The Lime-e[60] made me think about the last time I rode a bike and why. It also made me think about my endless battles and failures with giving up smoking and losing weight. (These are the two areas at which many self-improvement concerns take aim.)

A little background. Smoking and obesity are both prevalent in my family. I am not pointing fingers or naming names.

Let's just say I have a genetic pre-disposition. I have tried every diet I can think of and even after once losing 60 pounds, I remain in a deadlocked struggle with the bulge.

Regarding smoking, I began on and off at the age of thirteen. I bought my first pack with a friend from a local mini mart. I told the clerk I needed it for a science project. She could not have cared less about my story and made the sale. (Thanks, lady. I hope the $0.25 in profit covers your conscience.)

My friend and I took our cigs into the woods in the Willowbrook section of Staten Island (I never said I was bright) and proceeded to smoke 1.5-2 cigarettes each. We both commented on the smooth flavor and told lies about our previous experiences. When I got home, I ran to the bathroom. I had read that cigarettes made your urine smell and I didn't want my parents to find out.

I didn't smoke much more until the middle of tenth grade when, out of nowhere, my mind told me I wanted a cigarette. I think my craving came from marketing and familial exposure. Regardless, I figured I was under stress and a good smoke would relax me and make me cool.

Over the years, I have endured a hate-hate relationship with cigarettes. No matter what, even when I quit (once for seven years), I always find a way back. Happy times, sad times, the urge to smoke follows me around like a stray cat. I am a prisoner and I hate myself for it. I hate how smoking makes me look, how it makes me smell, and most of all, how it hurts my family.

Since I am someone who spends his days looking for opportunities to improve, being a prisoner of both weight and tobacco is unacceptable. I am determined to kick the issues to the curb once and for all.

In pursuit of these goals, I have historically gone the same route with weight loss as I did with smoking. I tried everything: fad diets, starvation, weight loss pills. Nothing worked. Right now, I have spent over $1,000 on cardboard disguised as "healthy, delicious food," have lost 15 pounds, gained back 20, and feel 10 years older than when I started.

I am not alone in my quest or in my pursuit of a healthier life. Consider these statistics.

- Smoking kills over 480,000 Americans a year. [61]
- 16% of people in my age bracket smoke. [62]
- Almost 16% of U.S. males smoke. [63]

Why then do we continue to fail? Why do we continue to buy into the hype trap? Even more, if we keep failing, why do we continue to try?

As I thought about these age-old questions, in the context of smoking and weight loss, I realized three things about myself. Whenever I try a new routine "destined" to fix one of those two issues, I always approach it the same way, with:

- Hope,
- An open mind (if I don't try, I cannot fail and learn), and
- The belief I will persevere – this time.

The problem is, when I am ready to act, the "fad" always seems to be conveniently available for me to begin now, now, now. Even when I know the fad will not work, it is often the least path of resistance for getting going. Not only is the fad there, but it also seems to talk to the 3 motivators listed above. Funny how that works.

Communications during times of immense change are one of the skills all organizations struggle with.

"What should I say?"

"How should I say it?"

"To whom should I say it?"

These are all questions that I hear from executives on every program I am a part of. It is not that they don't know how to speak but rather, with so much emotion circulating, how do you know what to say to strike the right chord and avoid offending people?

To be sure, these are complicated questions that often require market research so to speak to understand the audience and tailor the messaging. Still, there are a few key ideas that I have gleaned over the years that may help.

First, it is important to recognize that sometimes waiting to say something is worse than saying anything half way decent.

During times of change, communication needs to be there and purposeful and present or else a fad, like negativity or misdirection, can easily take its place. These bad vibes are like poison and often seem to talk to the basest of emotions and can quickly derail you from success. Once you are on a bad diet, no amount of exercise (e.g. more reporting, more hours etc.) will get you out. While the fad may give us immediate progress (at least it seems so), we sacrifice a strong foundation and ultimately crumble under the weight of the change.

Funny thing about communicating effectively in my world of corporate communications: sometimes we focus so much on making the language pretty that we miss the entire point of the message; to just fill the void and say something.

That's why Agile works for so many. Agile's processes force people to speak up. If you can't get something done and you say nothing, it is clearly on you.

Another idea for faster, effective communications goes back to the lessons in Chapter 9 around leadership. If you take the time to identify your core message and ensure that it is inspiring, you will often find a more receptive audience, especially when communicated with the Transformational Language mentioned in the last chapter.

To make a core message inspiring, I always like to "borrow" from the tried and true. Common themes include:

- The underdog
- The diamond in the rough
- Hope

Hope is one of my favorites. It is often in the media but not as frequently (at least overtly) in the corporate world. This is a shame because like love, hope is a universal idea – everyone can relate to it. No one longs for despair; no one wants to cling to the idea, "It will *never ever happen.*" Without hope, we would never invest in or pursue our dreams. Without hope for a greater future together, why would any of us get married or have children? When times are bad, why do we go on? Because we have hope that situations and circumstances will improve.

Even when people say they just want the facts, the reality is they want a message that gives them hope, something in which they can believe.

Making sure you encourage an open "test, act, and improve" mindset. You always want a call to action. You do not want a fad solution to creep in while your people figure out how to mobilize. When the test and act operate while looking through the lens of the single, simple, inspiring (hopeful) core message, your empowered team is unlikely to run amok.

Very powerful stuff indeed. When used properly and in this focused way, communications can lead to serious Transformation Arbitrage.

What's more, by using communication properly, a change leader can reinforce a new attitude and culture destined to grow deep and lasting roots extending well beyond the initial goal of the project. The culture will have been planted and reinforced through transformation and delivery – realities beyond valuable whether in your personal or professional lives.

Since we are here, some final thoughts on the importance of test and act when finding your communication voice.

I once interviewed with the Chief Strategy Officer of a major insurance company. It went great until his final question.

After discussing my qualifications and how I could help them win on their massive project, he asked me, "Do you ever fail?"

Shocked, I gave what I thought was a classic answer. Something like, "Yes, but I learn and correct."

I got the job and we had a super successful project. Still the question niggled at me like an itchy spot in the middle of the back. Of course, we all fail. Why would the CSO have assumed otherwise?

It took me a while, but I figured it out. In a very clever and socially acceptable way, the CSO was asking, "I know your track record sounds amazing, but has it made you a cocky asshole who can't see issues and adapt?"

Brilliant question. Permit me to answer this question more fully.

Yes, I fail all the time, but my failures have very little impact because my method is to:
- Test quickly
- Be very transparent throughout,
  - Work continually and closely with my customer to learn and adapt together

Testing forces failure and results in faster success because I am unafraid to be called out. I encourage input and work closely with teams to make sure the right message lands – and sticks. I have reduced the time and cost of implementation (of things like new functions) to mere fractions of what I have seen from my competition. So yes, I fail. I fail a lot. But my failure equals your success.

As you embark on your own controlled failures, some ideas to consider:
- Fail frequently
- Fail openly
- Fail up

The open, participatory nature of Kinetic Transformation's engineered failures is built on the idea of communal failure where everyone shares the risk...hears the feedback...and enjoys the credit. No one gets defensive as we cut through the noise and learn together. The process makes the team smarter and more self-sustaining, a very groovy thing for organizations looking to pivot and upskill fast.

The same holds true when trying to get in shape. If you have a training buddy, you are probably more likely to work out, find failure, and ultimately succeed. People need people and when one in our community stubs a toe, we all wince. As the famous Bible verse states: *ish echad b'lev echad* (one person, one heart).

Think about a gameshow that uses the accuracy of prices for products to determine success. Contestants poll the audience but the people in the seats are wrong as often as they are right, so why does "Martha from Des Moines" search the crowd for help on the price of a Whirlpool washer/dryer? Because when she does, she feels better about her decision.[64] If the "Wisdom of Crowds" has taught us anything, a bunch of "someones" knows more than we know alone.

Failing up is a concept I learned from my father. The idea is, it does not matter if you fail, as long as you are always growing and learning from the failure. This makes failure less accusatory and more desired. As an organization gets comfortable viewing failure in this way, massive communal learning can occur.

I guess this last point is a big reason why I will never stop trying to lose weight and quit smoking. While I can't promise that I won't be overweight or pick up that Marlboro again, I will never stop trying, adapting and improving my approach. Every day I quit means better health. Even if I relapse a few weeks later. In this way everything is a win so why not try?

My thoughts exactly.

Key Takeaways:

- Sometimes waiting to say something is worse than saying nothing

- During times of change, communication needs to be there, be purposeful and be present or else a fad, like negativity or misdirection, can easily take its place
- To make a core message inspiring, don't be afraid to "borrow" from the tried and true
    o The underdog
    o The diamond in the rough
    o Hope
- Always practice communication communally. Don't develop it in a vacuum

Section 4: Survive

It's funny, although I have had a truly unique career – and I am proud of it – I would argue that in some ways, my professional life has caused some of the worst pain in my life. As an entrepreneur trapped in a working stiff's clothes, the first 20 years of my career were spent hopping from job to job in the hopes of capturing ever-elusive satisfaction.

When we are young, we are all told to "do something we love" or focus on the "important things" like family and friends rather than money. Yet, the older I get the hollower the words ring. Without money (or at least a feeling of financial security), I have found it virtually impossible to enjoy the other fine aspects of my life.

As we now turn to a focus on my career working for the man, the only title I could think of for this section was: "Survive."

Given the time I invested in myself and the hours I spent at work, I can honestly say that for a long time the juice was not worth the squeeze. Imagine investing in a new Ferrari only to have the engine blow on the way home. That's how my life felt.

I share this bleak assessment with you to illustrate two important lessons. First, it is never impossible to turn it all around. Like I explained in Section 1, there is always a way to take control of even the most fundamental aspects of our lives. By focusing on understanding the big things and making some tweaks (such as to your surroundings) you can make big adjustments without reinventing the wheel.

But the there is also another lesson to be learned from the story of my early career. No matter what you do in life, if you are not happy with your lot, you will never be content. An adage from my culture stands the test of time: *azehu ashir, who b'sameach b'chelko.* ("What is wealth? He who is happy with his portion.") No matter how hard you work or what you accomplish, if you are unhappy with your portion, life will slog past you like bleak scenery on a desert highway.

Sadly, I see this principle play out in companies all over the world to their fantastic detriment. Some companies invest millions to fix something that ain't broke; others make management changes for no other reason than a desire to "refresh." Dissatisfaction comes in many forms and often prompts the wrong kind of action.

Recently I was working with a wonderful private equity portfolio company. The organization had experienced massive growth and was well on its way to even more success. I was asked to help transform how the employees worked – there had been a lot of squabbling and inefficiency. Despite the bottom-line success, the company was positioned to fail.

After a few weeks on the job it became apparent the issue was – and here is a highly-technical industry phrase – pure, unadulterated bullshit. Pardon the expression but the issues were 90% noise. Cut through all the bickering and complaining about not getting things done. The company had no metrics or data to measure success. What's more, the leadership team could not even agree what success was. How can you "win" when no one know what "winning" looks like?

In under three months, I established a structure that began moving the organization towards a more data oriented, responsive enterprise. This included refining their global operation into manageable pieces, implementing a brand-new strategic planning process, and a new leadership interaction model designed to identify, escalate, and resolve issues in under forty-eight hours. An amazing feat for any company, especially this one.

The crowning jewel of our achievements was the stand up of a new project intake process. For those who may be less familiar, large companies struggle with how to spend their money (rich people problems, I know). Deciding to have a strategy or vision from the top and how to translate it into action is a whole other story. Good companies will solicit ideas for projects intended, in a perfect world, to align to the higher strategy. These projects are gathered and validated with a business case to provide the costs and possible resulting benefits. The best management teams take these business cases, bump them up against each other, and decide where to invest their limited resources. This should be an annual process. The larger the company, the more ideas and the more difficult to maintain.

Such a strategic planning process is not simple, and no company does it perfectly. However, in this case, we killed it. Through Simpel's Kinetic Transformation Philosophy, we stood up a brand-new process, rolled it out globally, and gathered roughly 300 solid projects. Compared to other companies of this size from my past, we did about twice what we'd anticipated. We also unlocked a large increase in capacity without adding a single resource!

At the end of the process not only did the company have a strategic planning process with clarity about where it needed to invest, but it also had a rough order of magnitude estimate[65] and clear articulation of the folks who were accountable for delivering these projects. We even developed reporting that would allow businesspeople to track where their projects were in the lifecycle so they could intervene early in the event of a loss of momentum.

The day before I was going to spike the ball on this achievement at a board meeting, the CEO called. Expecting hearty congratulations, I answered with a cheery, "This is Nathan."

"Nathan, this is 'Joseph.' What the *fuck* is going on? Everyone is complaining about the process – it's overengineered and not working.

With the eloquence of Winston Churchill, I responded, "Huh?"

"We need to have an emergency meeting with the C-suite ASAP to discuss and address."

Click.

How could this have happened? How could I have been so off base?

The next day I presented the outcomes, a smashing success. No one posed a question I could not answer. The team was now empowered to deliver in an expeditious way the company had not experienced in its 100+ year existence. The leadership was speechless with excitement.

After the dust had settled, I met with the C-Suite. Instead of hearing how great things were, I listened to all manner of nonsensical complaints.

"The process is overengineered," the CEO said again.

"What do we do next?" the Chief Technology Officer said.

After about ten minutes, I had to jump in.

"How do you know?" I asked. "How do you know this is true? My data shows we exceeded my statement of work many times over, we have a clear plan of what to do next, and people are working faster and more efficiently than ever before. So, how do you know something is wrong?"

The CEO spoke up. "Our people are still not working efficiently. Our capacity is not maximized."

I repeated my question. "How do you know?"

Silence.

The company had always operated with an attitude of infallibility and when faced with simple questions to validate what they "just knew," they could not answer.

Seizing the momentum, I said, "Maybe the problem is there is no problem and we just need to get back to work."

The mood shifted like a change in wind direction. Eventually, the company refined its corporate strategy, removed the noise makers, and emerged a much happier and far more successful organization.

I see similar scenarios all the time – a sad reality when reworking a corporate culture. Sometimes people must accept that things are good and go with it. The key is always to make sure you use clear metrics and data to tell the story – always reassure yourself with the facts before heading toward the lifeboats.

It took me more than twenty years to know what I really wanted. When I did, I realized who I was and where I wanted to go. Armed with a new understanding, I gathered data from my career. When I put everything together, the story read very differently. I am no longer a failure but an artist.

Instead of the sad saga of the loser, I saw the story of an adventurer looking for happiness. There was love, treasure, and wonderment along the way. Of course, there were also traps and enemies, but in the end, I slayed the dragon, and carried away the treasure: happiness with who I am and what I have.

Now that's a tale worth telling.

Key Takeaways:

- It is never impossible to turn a situation around. As the famous Chinese proverb states "a journey of a thousand miles begins with a single step"
- If you are not happy with your lot, you will never be content. Take the time to write down what truly makes you happy and then see if your actions are aligned. This can lead to a happier life but also a better outcome through change
- Sometimes people must accept that things are good and go with it. Just be sure to use metrics and data to validate

CHAPTER 13: EVERYONE'S A SALESPERSON

I will never forget my first real job.

I was twenty and had just gotten married. My wife and I were settling into our first apartment, a one-bedroom. Both of us were going to school and then, in an instant, everything changed.

"I have some news for you," my wife said one morning. "We are going to have a baby."

The shock and excitement of becoming a dad settled in. When they did, fear tapped me on the shoulder. I had always wanted a family, but I was barely halfway through college.

The days pressed on and the reality grew (as evidenced by my wife's ever-expanding belly). I realized I needed a job.

But without a college degree, how?

After spending days locked in an office the size of my closet, I felt hopeless. I'd sent out hundreds of resumes and not gotten a single call. What would I do? How would we survive?

Working at McDonald's loomed ever larger in my reality. I bit the bullet and asked my father for advice. (Yeah, the same guy who told me when I was super depressed to shut the f-up and be productive.)

I mustered the courage, dialed the digits and, after a few forced moments of small talk, filled him in.

"Well, you're not going to believe it," I said. "I am going to be a father."

"Congratulations," he replied. "Are you excited?"

"Well, that's the thing. Yes, but I am frightened about how we are going to afford it. Life is expensive, and I can't seem to find a job."

In a flash, the great Dr. Gampel from the Bronx, New York, sprang into action. Without hesitation he replied, "Did you knock on every door?"

I said, "What? Are you kidding me? Knock on every door? Who does that?"

"Well," my father said, "until you are ready to be a man and do whatever it takes for your family, leave me the hell alone."

The phone went dead.

The conversation left me bewildered and angry but like everything else my father did, it was solid – some of the best advice I ever received. The truth dawned – no one would fight for my family more than me and unless I was unafraid to take every chance to succeed, I could not blame anyone else for my failure or fear. So, I mustered my courage and pounded on every door I could find.

After a few days, I scored my first job – a junior salesperson for a small, up and coming mortgage brokerage house.

In the early days of the boom of the 2000s, the mortgage industry was the place to be if you wanted to make big bucks. The founder of my first company had created a tele-sales division where inexperienced hires could learn to use the company's lead system and handle cold calling while more seasoned brokers focused on closing deals.

I did the math; the concept was brilliant. Even assuming high costs like real estate, computers, etc., all you needed was for one tele-salesperson to set up a single deal and it would pay for the entire group of 10 or so professionals. The company already owned the building, so space presented no issue. The company's sweet little sales generation arm worked like a charm and today the business is one of the largest mortgage brokers in the country.

From the very beginning, I realized how difficult it is to succeed at sales. Yes, you can learn to be a good salesperson, but it takes a lot of work. They are worth their weight in gold and should be appreciated and rewarded. The best salespeople develop a repository of skills. Almost all of them share certain gifts. They:

- Do not waste time
- Are always prepared with an answer
- Make the customer comfortable and confident
- Never leave without a follow up
- Never take rejection personally

Guess what – I had "it."

I was a whiz-bang on the phone. I dialed like a man on a Harley going 90 miles per hour with his hair on fire.

When a perspective client answered, I launched with my pitch, which included key questions to ferret out if the target was a player or a nobody. Not wasting time also meant I mined the company's deal system for as much intel about the prospect as possible. I had my presentation down to three or four key datapoints. I was *The Natural*.[66]

In what seemed like no time, I had multiple prospects meeting with me. I brought some brokers along for the ride and was gaining traction. The environment favored fast talking deal makers and was tailor-made for a guy (me) working full-time during the day and attending college at night. Motivation + a little (very little) knowledge + a big mouth = success.

During a meeting where the CEO was talking about sales and targeting, I spoke up with some suggestions I had gleaned from my evening college classes. Full disclosure, I'd lifted a few buzzwords from an article in the morning paper – but, hey, it worked. The boss was impressed. Within a few days (in a one-on-one), he explained the company was growing fast and needed someone to take on marketing. Of course, I jumped at the opportunity and declared myself "Director of Marketing." No one objected.

The title stuck and there you go.

My role only lasted a few months. In retrospect, the crazy part is – I was good. Without any knowledge or experience, I organized a marketing department including an inventory of artifacts. I also had a bunch of PR highlights like getting the company a full-page spread in the *NY Times* Real Estate section including an interview with the Chairman. I even created the logo the company uses to this very day. (There have been minor modifications over the last two decades, but the logo is essentially what I put together.)

Perhaps my crowning achievement was the introduction of a new idea: a website. It was the start of the dot-com boom and websites were all the rage. Even with my lack of significant experience, I found a web designer (very short supply in those days), a writer, and a marketer and launched the first website in the company's history.

I even convinced the CEO to look at the website not only as a marketing tool but also as a place on which we could generate business. My idea was to solicit information from clients and then provide indicative pricing on deals from relationship banks. Today this may seem like a passé idea but back then it was revolutionary.

Unfortunately for me, my time in this prestigious role was not long. The dot.com bubble burst and the market collapsed. Panic landed with a thud and my burgeoning marketing dream was over. Only hard sales remained, and I was left twisting slowly in the wind.

I have experienced my fair share of pain – lived through some of the worst boom-and-bust cycles in the history of the world (dot.com, Great Recession, the Covid-19 crisis). I have been on both sides – the guy laid off and the guy advising companies to give someone the bad news.

During a downsizing, you always hear the same advice.

"Keep your head down."

"Don't make waves."

In the end, I can tell you nothing works. By the time a

company starts filling in pink slips, the die is cast. If a division or group or individual is on a list, his or her name appears in indelible ink. Hiding or trying to appease the process does not work. When a company decides to cut costs, short-term actions driven by fear are useless. Your time is up, and there is nothing you can do about it.

I know how hard it can be. Being fired punches you in the gut and the questions will not stop.

"Am I a loser?"

"Am I a failure?"

"Will I ever work again?"

Picking yourself back up is hard especially when you are knocked down many times, but I guess that's why I have always appreciated salespeople so much. Rejection is not a rare occurrence in their line of work; it happens daily. Yet the best pick themselves up with such speed that they are often already on to the next deal before others in the room even know what happened. This instinct and adaptability is so vital to success, especially during transformational times.

As my consulting practice has grown, the importance of always having an answer has only increased in significance. Sometimes you do not have the answer and need an answer for that. It's hard! But when you are confident, comfortable, and flexible in how you approach questions, the person asking the question relaxes and is more likely to buy.

Oh – you will be rejected. If you cannot handle being turned down, you will never make it in sales or life. Accept the reality and make the pitch anyway.

Looking back on it, sure, my dad was harsh. And the colliding aspects of quick accomplishment and a jaw-dropping dismissal made my first job a rough experience. Over the years, I came to know this sting more times than I can count, and I have felt hopeless more times than I care to say.

But I never let circumstances drag me to the bottom of the pool because I knew two things about sales...

...never take "no" as the ultimate answer...

...and never quit selling yourself.

Key Takeaways:

•   We can all benefit from good sales skills, especially during times of immense change
•   No one will sell you harder and better than you sell yourself. Especially when things are in flux, always remember the power is in your hands
•   Key attributes from sales that we can all benefit from include:

        o   Not wasting time
        o   Always having an answer
        o   Making the customer comfortable
        o   Making the customer confident
        o   Never leaving without a follow up
        o   Never taking rejection personally

CHAPTER 14: ALL TRANSFORMATIONS ARE PROJECTS BUT NOT ALL PROJECTS ARE TRANSFORMATIONAL

If there is a silver lining to being laid off; you find it by getting your next job. My dad likes to say, "You never know when it is going to happen but if you keep going, it always seems to happen when you need it most."

After I left the mortgage brokerage house, I was fortunate enough to land a position with a leading Fortune 500 financial services firm. Here's where I also worked on my initial broad-based transformational program. I joined the team as an analyst focused on delivering reporting for the company's middle market business.

I was a bit of a Jack of all trades, but I rose quickly to an informal management level. The company had a cool idea. To encourage middle tier companies to accept their financial products, they provided a program whereby partners received a percentage of the fees they paid in the form of a cooperative marketing arrangement – a neat deal to build cooperation and loyalty in the market, but a hell of a program to manage.

Back in those days, reporting was limited, and Excel had a nasty habit of crashing. You can imagine that managing a budget line for thousands of customers nationwide was ridiculously inefficient. But, with tens of millions of dollars in wasted marketing opportunity sitting on the books, the company had to stay on top of things. It had four regional analysts spread throughout the country who managed budget lines and reported to their regional VPs.

Quickly realizing the inherent inefficiency of the structure, I started to provide roll up reporting. Leaders liked the simplicity so much that I soon became the central funnel for data requests. I found myself in meetings with senior VPs (and above) where I shared ideas and worked to move things forward.

One day, our senior VP decided we needed to do away with the albatross of a program by reengineering the entire portfolio. Though no small feat, he was determined to execute the change without the loss of a single customer. To give some perspective – imagine thousands upon thousands of customers. Some received back a few dollars in cash; others got hundreds of thousands. Some merchants were very small, and others numbered among the largest brand names in the world. In some cases, the funds we provided through the initiative made up the clients' entire annual marketing outlay. How could we "disappear the program" without any defections?

I was the central analyst; I quickly emerged as a leader. I helped organize my colleagues and provided direction so we could implement the broader change strategy. Ultimately, we saved the company over $20 million in run rate and were awarded the company's highest honor. Quite a groovy thing to get a fat bonus and have dinner with the global CEO in my first year on the job.

So why did this program, which transformed how the company interacted with its customers, succeed? It began with the recognition that it was a transformation, not a project.

As I state in the white paper, *Agile for Transformations, the Basis for Just In Time Staffing,* The Simpel Transformation Test defines a Transformational Initiative as a project that: 1) is management sponsored; 2) operates outside of BAU[67]; 3) requires a heavy investment of time, money or resources; 4) is quantifiable; and 5) distinctly changes operating norms.

Sometimes in life and in business we are faced with challenges so big, we don't know where to begin. This initial feeling of anxiety often propels us down the wrong track. Once inertia sets in, people get discouraged, frustrated, and angry, which ultimately leads to resistance and failure. To me, a good way to ward off problems is to put any change situation into perspective as quickly as possible. Here is where the test comes in.

Many times, clients believe they are undergoing a transformation when, in fact, they are simply facing a complicated project. Why the distinction? Because it drives everything from the work team, to the approach to how funds are invested and the anticipated outcome(s).

A project - even a complex one - is clearly finite and tends to flow in a linear fashion, e.g. I do "x," then "y," and finally "z," which leads to "Outcome 123." This in turn means that execution is driven by a more direct approach with an emphasis on getting it done quickly and efficiently with minimal disruption to business as usual. Work is done at the worker level, compartmentalized by function or functions playing their part with reporting used to keep things moving and in line.

A transformational initiative, however, might take different paths and the result might not be what you initially envisioned. You think you are out to change your culture when in fact the root cause lies in the need to change your entire staffing model. Successful transformation programs are ones where leadership realizes the need for insight, understands the likelihood of change, and is flexible enough to accept it.

Transformational initiatives also tend to result in deep, lasting change as opposed to a more "modular" alteration like installing a new piece of software. Therefore, transformational projects often include initiatives like outsourcing or redesigning a target operating model. These types of programs are dynamic and permanently impact how an organization does business. They can be growth and/or turn around oriented. Unlike a project designed to get it done as quickly and inexpensively as possible, a transformation wants to be quick and inexpensive but must also be sustainable to achieve success. When you drive people and force them to deliver faster until they burn out and are replaced, it is far more difficult to change how someone works and why.

Transformational initiatives are often made up of discreet projects that are part of a broader effort or strategy. For example, I may want to change my operating model and outsource large swaths of what I do. Such an effort will include projects like implementing a new workflow (business process management) tool or training future employees. Alone, these steps would be finite initiatives but taken together, they form a broader, more strategic view of things designed to impact how the business operates into the future.

Differentiating between transformational initiatives and simple projects proves critical when trying to manage time or to control our emotions on a personal level.

My wife was recently involved in a car accident. Some jerk bumped her while merging onto the highway during rush hour. The asshole drove away and left her holding the bag.

When I heard about the accident, a flood of questions and emotions hit me. Was my wife okay? Did my wife need to see a doctor? Was the car demolished? How hard would it be to fix? Would we need to be without a car for a few days? Will my insurance premium go up?

The old me would have freaked out and been in a bad mood all day. I would have gotten it all done but believe me, it would not have been pleasant. However, this time, I subdivided everything into a series of tasks. The approach allowed me to comfort my wife and to attend to all the necessary actions in good order. Nothing was overwhelming and it all got done faster than it would have had my younger self been in charge.

Why? Because I approached the situation as something with a beginning, an end, and very simple goals in between. Everything started with the most important factor: ensure the wife is safe. After that, the tasks flowed like water going downhill.

At the financial services company, I experienced a transformational program first-hand. Sure, we had to develop analyses and messaging for our clients but what made it transformational was that the company was changing how it fundamentally interacted with its customers. This transformation impacted everything from customer experience to opportunities for future sales. All the pieces of the program needed to work together to deliver transformation seamlessly.

During the process, I saw how a world class organization prioritized the work and the team. I learned how leadership recognized the significance of the change and set aspirational rules to govern the work (from the beginning). The rules included statements like, "I don't care how much we can save; we will not lose a single customer during this project." The work team and the organization were aligned at a higher, strategic level, which set the tone for how the effort ran and how all our individual projects worked together to deliver on a higher-level dream.

Perspective helps in both business and life. Sometimes it is as simple as stopping, recognizing where you are, and then organizing your approach. Once you do this, you will be surprised how quickly things fall into place.

Key Takeaways:

- All transformations are projects but not all projects are transformational
- This distinction drives everything from the work team, to the approach to how funds are invested and the anticipated outcome(s)
- Projects are initiatives with beginnings, end-

ings and outcomes. They can be very large or very small but the goal and timeline are usually clear

• The Simpel Transformation Test defines a Transformational Initiative as a project that:

1) Is management sponsored

2) Operates outside of BAU

3) Requires an investment

4) Has quantifiable outcomes

5) Distinctly changes operating norms

• Transformations result in clear changes to who you are and how you operate. The emphasis on managing change during delivery is one reason transformations require a different approach and thought process than standard projects

CHAPTER 15: ACING THE BASICS – THE REAL GOAL OF DIGITAL TRANSFORMATION

(WARNING: This chapter details the business-centric concepts behind digital transformation. Without it, this work would be incomplete. For those less interested in the technical, business side of change, consider skipping.)

I always loved the phrase "ace the basics." I remember the first time I heard it. I was working at one of the largest banks in the world as a product manager hired to develop a corporate banking market for endowments, foundations and not for profit healthcare companies. I was very young, freshly laid off during the financial crisis, and new to a job about which I knew nothing.

In a bid to open a new market, a senior leader at the bank hired one of the most prestigious strategy firms to tell her which market to approach and what to sell. Of course, the firm had beautifully crafted slides with an impressive business case designed to validate a massive investment. The only issue? Neither the leader nor the firm understood the business. They didn't take the time to speak to people in the market and so they missed how difficult the business was to enter. There was little differentiation among a deeply entrenched oligopoly. In addition, the clients were more socially minded and did not want to engage with players who had not proven their support of their mission over time. The effort was woefully underinvested and doomed to fail from the start.

But the slides sure looked great.

Anyway, during this time my more creative, analytical skills were beginning to emerge. Like a newly aware Jedi trainee, I gravitated to the issues and enjoyed offering my unsolicited opinion about how to solve every problem.

For whatever reason, people were listening and valuing my opinion.

One day, a gentleman we'll call "Gary" (for no other reason other than it is the first name to pop in my head) reached out to me for a conversation. Gary was leading an internal initiative designed to improve performance and he heard I had ideas and would be "happy to share."

Prideful and in my best shirt and tie (yes, even I wore a tie then), I met with Gary to discuss my opinions. It was a very good exchange, professionally led, and it ran the gamut. We discussed my thoughts on technology, process, people, and organization.

After a few weeks, Gary reached out again to share his findings. His presentation opened very professionally with the first key: our company would benefit from "acing the basics." I loved the phrase. I thought, *How relevant.* I was barking about "issues" when I should have said the bank had lost focus on the basics of business and operations. They were working on their "spin move" when they should have been "blocking and tackling."

Over the course of countless high-priced consulting engagements, I always muse how frequently it is a loss of focus on the basics, that foretell disaster. I'm talking about "101" stuff – payroll processing, basic reporting, review meetings, etc. They are not sexy but we either do them or perish!

With businesses investing heavily on modernization and

improving fundamental aspects of their operations in recent years, acing the basics suddenly became a big "thing." In the aftermath of the 2008 financial crisis, banks struggled to implement changes to processes and systems arising out of new regulations. These projects forced to the surface the challenges of working with decades' old banking technology. The more that regulations demanded small system changes (such as adding a data field here or there) to core or basic systems, the more the costs increased until they reached a tipping point. (FATCA[68] anyone?) This realization was a key contributor to the consulting gold rush that became known as "digital transformation."

What began as a catchy buzzword often used interchangeably with another hot word, "disruption," eventually morphed into a new way of approaching how companies operate in today's world.

Like the word "smoothie," the term "Digital Transformation" seemed to represent an unending number of initiatives intended to modernize key aspects of a business by jumping from point A to point D.

"Don't like how your bank works? Use the latest technology to stand up a new, digital bank alongside it."

"Is your technology infrastructure clunky and outdated? Use an Agile based Digital Transformation approach to quick-change it."

Digital Transformation became so amorphous and lucrative that it almost lost all meaning. I can't tell you how many "experts" I spoke to who could not adequately describe what made the change digital and why it was important. All they knew was that it was "important," and companies were willing to pay through the nose for it. Don't believe me? See if you can dig up marketing collateral between 2010-2015. Compare two different companies' interpretations and you will see right away; no one knew what they were talking about.

In my experience, when companies say "Digital Transformation" what they really mean is dramatically modernizing core aspects of a business using an Agile approach.

Digital Transformation Initiatives tend to focus on:
- External interactions,
- Internal simplification, and
- Cross functionalization.

External Interactions

External interactions involve getting back to the basics of customer service through technology.

Once upon a time, your banker knew you. Then everything changed.

In the '80s and '90s, the stock market exploded, companies got rich, and megadeal after megadeal was sold to the public. It was the age of rapid American expansion and technological revolution. Our lives as consumers were supposed to get better.

Unfortunately, the pressures of never-ending revenue and expense control got to the new uber companies and "making the deal work" gained priority over the customer. Legacy systems and processes were not built to handle the new, massive influx of customers and rather than investing in full integration or introducing new, complicated technology, companies simply "made it work" with more M&A.

At the same time, the growth of the internet made it easier for customers to find new options. The bigger the company grew, the more diverse its product offering and the more complicated it became for customers to interact with and understand.

Some companies became so unwieldy that even the most fundamental aspect of any business, talking to a customer, became an industry unto itself.

Around this time, a new marketing *term du jour* appeared. "Omni-channel marketing" was a singular way of describing how a company consistently speaks to a customer via multiple channels such as web, mobile, print, etc. Keeping the message consistent across the board became a separate job. Can you imagine? A job to oversee the job of simply talking to a customer? Add on to that the growth of other experience improvement roles such as "customer specialists" whose role in many companies was to "own the end-to-end interaction with the customer" and you can see the bloat and confusion from a mile away.

No wonder customer loyalty is such a problem. If you can't easily speak to your customer about your product, why would anyone want to stay?

As a response, companies turned to big data. "Data crack" (such as gathering limitless amounts of data) became the norm. In turn, this led to another issue: now that we have all this data, what do we do with it? Of course, another cottage industry sprang to life: data analysis and reporting.

After a few years and lots of money, it all came together in today's optimized digital organization. Data startups emerged, one after another, to fill gaps. Companies grew more savvy about the value of data and how to use it in a more fluid way such as through sophisticated reporting and reporting tools. Data became actionable and informative, especially when supported by refined processes and teams accustomed to working in a more fluid or Agile manner.

Digital Transformation in the context of external interactions is about designing systems, creating processes, and using data to enhance what the customer experiences when interacting with the company (also known as "the customer journey"). The goal is to create a seamless, consistent interaction with the least amount of friction or complication while yielding the maximum amount of insight about the customer as he/she moves from sale to service.

Internal Simplification

Following the customer interaction continuum, once the customer buys via a digitally enhanced channel, servicing the client moves to what is referred to as "the middle and back office." Here's where a company's operations and core systems spring into action. This is the gnarly stuff you as the customer don't see. Frankly, companies emphatically don't want you to see it.

You would not believe how complicated it can be.

Consider the stock brokerage statement you receive monthly. You would not believe how many thousands of people that little piece of paper represents. From the trader or system that executes and properly books your trades, to the complex banking systems that move the money and properly records it, to the printing machines running all night to print out the statement and make sure it is mailed to the right place every month – the process is mammoth. Ignorance of all this is truly bliss, believe me.

After the fallout of the Great Recession, I found myself reengineering some of the largest mortgage servicers in the world. These mega banks were responsible for everything from ensuring client payments to document storage for what is perhaps the most important financial asset for most families. Basic stuff, right? You'd be shocked by how often no one could find a customer's document or answer basic questions. In the rush to grow, grow, grow, the companies had forgotten about the basics.

With millions of customers representing hundreds of billions of dollars in loans, a loss of focus on the basics nearly destroyed the world's economy. All the accumulated scotch tape and bubble gum began to weigh things down in inefficiency and sadly, fraud.

Unfortunately for the banks, the government stepped in – the financial institutions had to comply, fast. It was impossible to fix all the basic interactions using traditional approaches. In response, under the banner of Digital Transformation, more Agile approaches to process redesign and system implementation came in vogue. The idea was to identify problematic areas and to replace the systems or processes with more scalable and flexible solutions.

For example, systems were historically mainframe based. Think of an enormous, all-knowing computer from which all data and functionality flowed. In the modern, digital world, a new concept known as "software as a service" popped up. Systems no longer required hosting on a client's infrastructure.

Instead, software would be hosted at a vendor and made accessible via a new concept known as "the cloud." Clients could get the latest updates and purchase only the functions they needed.

Internal simplification also grew in other areas of a company such as the marketing function where the reams of data collected during the external interactions became useable data to support better and more targeted outreach. This supported more personalized customer interactions and of course, more sales.

How about the finance function? Through Digital Transformation, whole, fundamental processes like those supporting "order to cash" were almost completely redefined. The result led to better and more accurate reporting and the opportunity to take advantage of lower-cost employee locations.

Cross Functionalization
Digital Transformation is also about changing how a company interacts across divisions. With the increasing pervasiveness of social media, companies have begun to realize the power of community and increased communications. Digitally Transformed companies recognize and implement tools designed to facilitate the basics of how people speak to each other, which results in, you guessed it, marked increases in efficiency, revenues, and creativity.

In my first job at a Fortune 500, email was pervasive. I know, I'm a dinosaur but it was amazing at the time. You no longer needed to call someone and waste time with chitchat. You could tap out a message and blast it out to whomever you wanted. You could even send important documents and programs.

As the digital revolution picked up steam, even a basic tool like email was improved and enhanced with tools like Slack. When I first heard of Slack and tools like it. I thought, *Dumb! It's just a more robust Instant Message – what's the big deal?*

Then, I used it.

I was working on a major global transformation at a

2,000+ person organization. The company wanted to experiment with a tool like Slack and I was instructed that adoption was one of my core goals.

At first everyone hated it. The tool was super annoying and hard to navigate.

"Where are my attachments?" was a common refrain.

No matter how loud the noise, refusing to use the tool was not an option. If you sent an email, a message from the program's sponsor was soon to follow. I was the email police and I hated it.

After a while something interesting began to happen. Messaging became a lot faster and informal. Yes, mistakes were sometimes made but the tool's group instant messaging format meant that everyone received timely messages quickly. Response times also sped up and accountability improved. People could no longer hide behind the excuse, "Oh, I was left off the distribution." Everyone knew everything and it became your responsibility to be in the know.

I can honestly say this simple tool – redefining something as basic as email – represented a key factor in the initiative's success.

As an organization grows, small things can morph into big problems. In running a small consulting outfit, I certainly find expense management tedious, but it is something I can dispatch in the space of one morning. When companies expand, routine tasks like this can grow into substantial drains on productivity. They can ruin a business.

Digital Transformation allows a business to modernize and to do so with speed. But beware of the buzz words. By its very nature Digital Transformation is dramatic, institutional change – it must be respected and treated appropriately.

To be successful, Digital Transformation requires the same flexibility and thoughtful approach as other Transformational Initiatives. You do not want to improve a small process here and there while you whiff on the opportunity to ace the basics of business in the 21st century.

Key Takeaways:

• "Digital Transformation" is a dramatic modernization of core aspects of a business often using an Agile approach
• Digital Transformation initiatives tend to focus on:
  o External interactions
  o Internal simplification
  o Cross functionalization
• When performing a Digital Transformation, don't forget that it is about more than just implementing new technology. It is a change in how you work and requires the same level of care as other transformational initiatives

CHAPTER 16: IN THE INTERVIEW, YOU ALWAYS KNOW

When I was a kid, people stood in awe of the Ivy League. I mean, don't get me wrong, when someone says, "I got my degree from Princeton," a hush still falls over the room. But, thirty years ago, if you got into an Ivy, you felt you were the smartest person in the room and destined for greatness.

The years progress and you learn there are no givens in life. I have seen Ivy Leaguers who made great impacts on society. But remember, 50% of folks in the Ivy League finish in the bottom half of their class. I also know men and women who have started at "no name schools" and gone on to find happiness, satisfaction, and for some, extreme wealth.

What do Richard Branson, Nicole Kidman, Aretha Franklin, Joe Lewis, and Quentin Tarantino all have in common? They all dropped out of high school.[69]

Education has changed radically – especially in the last decade. At one end, it continues to be prohibitively expensive. But an ever-expanding community college scene and accessible online education touches more people every day. Yes, going to Harvard or Brown or Cornell or Yale is very cool – and a great achievement. But we are all better served by attending the program that is right for us. "Ivy or bust" sets a lot of people up for disappointment.

Over the last two years, my family has geared up to support our daughter as she applied to college. Rebecca has always been "that awesome kid." So, it came as a shock to me when she announced her decision to apply to music colleges. In my strongest, old-school, Staten Island, "I love you and respect you, but I am your dad and know best" voice, I asked, "Don't you want to be a lawyer?"

Rebecca looked straight at me with her piercing blue eyes and said, "No, I am a singer and a businesswoman. That's what I love and where I will flourish. I want to attend a college that specializes in the music business, so I will have the best shot of getting into the industry".

My initial reaction was to yell, then stomp away. Then I punched in some numbers.

Top tier schools run $75-large, per year ($300,000 – if she finished a degree in the traditional eight semesters). Add incidentals and law school and I was going to be well over half-a-mil in the hole before my daughter earned her first nickel as a barrister.

The numbers are mind boggling – especially if (are you listening parents?) *she did not want to be an attorney!*

Boom! My eyes were opened as never before, and I saw the new business model for college. Rather than aspiring to a single standard (Ivy or bust), schools were developing more targeted approaches to education. With differentiation comes more opportunity to focus on niche areas (like music business in Rebecca's case). With this focus, the student has a higher likelihood to enter the career of their choosing and as the saying goes, when you are happy you are far more likely to succeed. Considering my own misadventures as an artist in the corporate world and you can see how true this rings true to me.

Rebecca's choice also offers a "co-op" program where soon-to-be young professionals learn – wait for it – how to get a job, arguably the most important life skill (and certainly on top of every parent's list of "What I want my kid to learn at college).

On the higher education landscape, customer interest shifted, and the business of universities is transforming itself in response.

Think back. When you were younger, how many adverts did you see for local colleges? Now they are as ubiquitous as car commercials. Online degrees continue to gain acceptance as employers begin to catch on to the realities of the cost of going to college. This is likely one of the most underappreciated and successful transformations in modern American business history.

Despite their lofty reputations, high-end schools that cling to the past will eventually find themselves in trouble. The world is changing – the customer base is always in flux – and companies (and yes, Dear Ole State U) must change as well.

Unfortunately, when I was younger, I did not have Rebecca's insight or courage. Instead of understanding myself, I spun my wheels and tried to find my "square self" into the round holes of everyone else's idea of achievement. With a little more discernment, I might still have moved around some, but I would have developed depth and gravitas sooner and saved myself (and those around me) a lot of pain.

I did not naturally fall into consulting as a profession. With degrees from smaller undergraduate and graduate schools, big name companies were not pounding on my door and asking my advice. Even when I managed to sneak my toes into the door of an Ivy League school, I was never part of "the Club." Getting anyone to talk to me was always a challenge.

My first job at a real consulting firm came by accident. I had been in the corporate world about eight years and had a fast-moving role for a leading global bank. Though my career was very bright, I have mentioned my misery. I hated the work I was doing. I despised my commute and I did not feel comfortable in the corporate environment.

Making matters worse, I had entered the world of banking while I was pursuing my MBA at night. When I finished, I started a second master's degree in Social Organization Psychology. I worked hard during the day to support my family and then pursued my academic interests in the evenings.

At the time, I was leading the development of a global product to service the newly emerging Exchange Traded Fund industry. I was responsible for overseeing a leading consultancy who was helping us figure it out. One night, I found myself in a conversation with one of the partners where I expressed my interest in pursuing a career in consulting. To my delight, the partner responded I should come work for them.

I could not believe my luck. The firm was in major growth mode, expanding from a traditional accounting/advisory-based consultancy to a supermarket provider of strategy to operations to IT. Hiring me was part of the firm's plan to connect the dots between newly acquired strategy practices and the traditional advisory practices. I would be a "super athlete" who could play both ways and help bridge the gap.

I still remember my first day. I was so confident that I would be partner in three years, I left and told my wife to be on the lookout for the classic, "Honey, I made partner" conversation when I got home.

My initial emotions were of excitement and amazement. I remember being so blown away by virtually everything, I loved it!

The haze of happiness continued until I completed my first project. Since I would be traveling, I was thrilled with the idea of staying in nice hotels, eating fun food on the road, and most of all, racking up the frequent flyer miles.

I was also thrilled about the prospect of seeing our amazing country. Except for my year abroad, I hadn't travelled much, and I was excited about all the people I would meet and the things I would experience. I even got to experience what 135 degrees feels like in the Texas sun.

Amazing.

I spent about nine months on the project and did very well. Even though I began by stepping on my team's toes and annoying my engagement manager, things turned around. I even got to visit my client's (one of the leading banks in the world) corporate headquarters in New York City and meet with the division's president.

At the end, I received a personal thank you from the day-to-day sponsor, someone I did not even think knew my name. It was cool and very exciting. But, like all things in my career to this point, the good times were not meant to last. Soon, I was very unhappy.

After we finished, while my potential was clear, things soon began to unravel. I had not consulted before and did not understand the fundamentals of managing a consulting engagement, especially at a large firm. Trying to catch up on 10 years of firm life while billing 2,000 hours a year proved a lot more difficult than I expected. Like so many others, the transition from years spent working in industry to a firm environment was a lot more difficult than expected.

Looking back on it now, I bear a lot of the blame. When I realized a trend forming, I should have left. The work was different from what I had anticipated – it was not me – and I did not fit.

Sometimes in transformation that's just how it is. We want to transform, to be better, but we don't adequately understand who we are, our resources and even if we truly know what we want.

That's why Kinetic Transformation engagements always begin with a thorough assessment of the 1) change 2) organization 3) people 4) leadership and 5) communications. By taking the time to develop a thorough, holistic understanding of the change and context of the environment where it is occurring, a transformation leader will have the data needed to properly construct the change effort and see it through.

This data is used to support creation of goals and provide structure for data capture. As the program rolls on, the data is also used to inform on the approach and validate direction.

But I wanted to be "an expert." I wanted to offer sage advice to high-end clients. Instead, the team-based approach of large projects put me in a very specific, focused box. I felt like I was always wearing a suit that did not quite fit. I had not learned "their way."

Sure, the clients liked me but, in the end, I was not working for the clients. I was working for the firm and I did not jive with their approach. Subsequently, I came across as disjointed and out of sync. I was ill-equipped to work with the team and to deliver the firm's approach – the one the clients had purchased.

Working for a large consulting firm was not me and was not aligned with what I wanted to do. While it was good for learning purposes, it was simply the wrong time in my career for learning on the job. Had I caught on earlier, I would have been happier. I could have developed Kinetic Transformation sooner and launched my firm. But, to quote C.S. Lewis, "There are far better things ahead than any we leave behind."[70]

Looking back on it now, I realize that, like my daughter, I should have first recognized who I was and then gone for the jobs. Had I done so I probably would have realized right away that at that point in my life, I would never be successful at these firms. Ironically, looking back on it now, I knew because of a conversation with a friend long ago.

Ten to fifteen years ago, I was attending night school and looking for a job in the corporate world – something that might pay real money. As resume after resume went out with no response, I grew increasingly desperate. My wife still speaks of the times I locked myself in the closet/office in our first apartment, often not coming out for a day or more. I sent out hundreds of resumes in the hope someone would call me back. It was pathetic.

One day I had some good news. I had an interview at a major company. I was so excited.

Focusing my nervous energy on preparation, I began to consume as much information as possible. I read every article I could find and surfed the internet like a madman.

On the day of the interview, I was ready. I turned on my best salesmanship and worked the hell out of the interviewers. I used my prepared list of insightful questions and smiled as proudly as I could.

After I left, I was on pins and needles. Unable to contain myself, I created a plan. I wrote thank you letters crafted to invite a response. I embellished the expressions of gratitude and asked the recipients to contact me with any further questions.

I got exactly zero responses.

What did I do wrong? Was I too aggressive?

Later that day I went out to dinner with a buddy. Don and I discussed my predicament.

"How do I know if this company likes me"? I asked with no expectation of a response.

"Should I just sit and worry or is there some way to know what's going to happen?"

Don's response was brilliant.

"In the interview," he said, "you always know."

He asked me if I had been comfortable?

"Yes," I replied.

"Did you like the company and do you want to work there"

"Yes."

"Then," he said, "you probably got the job."

And – I did.

Don, not an outwardly emotional person, had tapped into a major idea. With rare exceptions (sociopaths and the like), deep down we always know when "he's just not that into you"[71] to repurpose a phrase.

We know it won't work.

While I can't tell you why we know or give you the magic recipe for using this information to avoid bad relationships, I can tell you that the concept touches on one of the core values of The Kinetic Transformation Philosophy: "It is all worthless without truth."

We all have defense mechanisms, and I am not trying to berate anyone, but if we are honest enough to push aside the BS and to see through our own defenses, we are all smart enough to anticipate most things coming before they happen. (Organization ESP) The trick is to learn how to be aware of the data, to be honest with ourselves, and to leap without paralyzing fear.

The moral of all of this... Never be afraid to be honest. Sure, you may not like the results in the short term, but I guarantee, the more you practice being honest, the easier it gets and the happier you will be overall.

A final thought: recently I realized that whenever I have discussions about important future events, like the state of the economy, there is always someone whose point of view begins with, "I am not a pessimist; I am a realist." They then proceed to explain why the most horrible outcome will occur and they are simply keeping it real.

Might I suggest a different approach? Why do people feel they come across as "honest" or "more truthful in their assessment of the data" by being negative? Instead, how about looking at the data, being objective and defaulting to "hey it may just work out" every once in a while?

Sad but true – it is easier to be pessimistic than to be an optimist. But how would a world full of pessimists look?

Would we have medications?

Would we have explorers?

Being honest is just that, being honest – sometimes a hard thing. Sometimes, like early in my career, you just fail and fail again – it's hard to get back up. Being honest means being unafraid to face hard truths and to pursue what you know is right. With a little practice you will see because...

...in the interview, you always know.

Key Takeaways:

• Never be afraid to be honest. You may not like the results in the short term, but the more you practice the easier it gets and the happier you will be

• Never be afraid to be an optimist. It is easy to think the worst will happen but optimism breads optimism and more positive outcomes

Section 5: Actualize

About four years ago, I founded my company for two reasons: necessity and desire. Despite my best efforts, I wasn't making it at a major firm. I was too much of an independent thinker – at every job, I was always "the sand in the gears". I was not getting any younger and I knew it would be impossible to compete with folks half my professional age. Too much time had passed. The learning curve involved in joining yet another group presented the business equivalent of scaling Everest. With three kids and a wife, I had no choice.

But I also *wanted* to sail my own ship. With a desire to return to the reasons I chose consulting at the beginning, I thought I could approach the craft from a different and innovative angle. My infatuation with the field of management consulting began when I was in law school, a destination I had never anticipated or intended. It just happened.

I was living in Brooklyn with my wife and our new baby daughter. We were happy with each other, but not so much with our apartment. Brooklyn was a little overwhelming for Sara.

Having recently completed my undergraduate degree, I was toiling away at a major financial services firm and studying for the GMAT in the evenings. Things were calm – but I was, per usual, miserable. Work held no allure or excitement. Even though I had no interest in the path I was traveling, I did not see a way out of the quagmire.

I know what you are thinking. *Really? What do you want, man? You were with one of the best companies – well, ever –and you were killing it.*

Although Gertrude Stein[72] once commented, "Whoever said money can't buy happiness simply didn't know where to go shopping," in truth, if you are not content, no amount of money will put a spring in your step or ease the ache in your heart. Nothing in my work made me special and I did not understand how I was going to impact anything with any significance.

I had applied to multiple business schools, but I was not

ready. I didn't know which program I should attempt or what I wanted if I were accepted. Luckily, the decision was made for me.

One day, I received a letter from a leading law school. Apparently, they were running a pilot program and admitting qualified students into a new program with the option of business school. Not only that, but they also offered a healthy scholarship. How could I say no? Packing our bags, we were off to beautiful southern New Jersey and our new life as "country bumpkins."

After the first year of what was supposed to be a four-year experience, a trio of things became clear:

- I would never be a lawyer,
- We loved Southern New Jersey, and,
- I needed a different kind of job.

While I did not blow the doors off law school, I landed a highly coveted day job at a major Philadelphia law firm with a partner who really liked me. The firm was on the move, and I could – sometimes – envision a career there. But I had to follow my heart, so I quit to focus on my M.B.A. studies and a career in the broader business world.

Thinking about what a "different kind of job" meant, my wife and I explored many, many options. For a time, I considered becoming a Navy SEAL. Yeah, me, 28 years old with asthma and two children swimming 500 yards, doing 80-100 pushups and an equal number of sit-ups, completing 10-20 pull-ups, and running 1.5 miles in – well – ever. (The preferred time is 9-10 minutes – like *that's* ever going to happen). All those things are *entrance* requirements – before you get to the living outdoors, blowing up stuff, and being shot at part.

So, I thought about "easier" options: the FBI and the CIA. When reality set in, I contemplated investment banking, securities, and market research.

One day I was speaking with a friend who had recently graduated Harvard Business School. He was working for one of the leading strategy firms. Fed up with the corporate world, and wanting to do something different, he started an international real estate company and made serious coin. I was fascinated and wanted to learn more.

Through *Wikipedia*, I discovered the larger field of management consulting and the story of James McKinsey.[73] Apparently, Mr. McKinsey started a specialty practice providing expert advice in his field. This practice ballooned into the billion-dollar industry we know today. The more I learned, the more interested I became. I never had the ability or desire to be a doctor but there was something to be said for using the accumulated knowledge of my academics in a more meaningful way.

As I daydreamed about how cool it would be to fly first class and meet with the leaders of industry over steaks and cigars, I knew I was hooked. Consulting fit the bill and I was all in.

My road to consulting was not easy. None of the big firms (or any firms of note) recruited at my school and no one wanted a law school dropout with an MBA from a school not in the Top 10. Still, I was undeterred. I created a targeting list of potential companies and worked my butt off, sending resumes, networking, and interviewing.

When I finally made it to the big leagues of management consulting via my relationship with the firm I was overseeing, I was certain I would make partner in three to five years (tops). After all, I had left a job where I was flying, demonstrated very strong sales skills, and had successfully overseen multiple consulting engagements. Most of all, I wanted it badly and, supported by Sara, was going to do whatever it took to get there.

Reflecting on why it did not work, perhaps the leading reason was that consulting was not what I thought. Working for the big firms was about selling massive, complicated projects that leveraged multiple leaders from different areas of the firm. While someone could emerge as a thought leader in a discipline, the climb took many years and was not something simple. I had invested in my education and I wanted to replicate Mr. McKinsey's success. I wanted to provide expertise and leverage my background to help leaders make better decisions. I thought I could help teams win but instead I felt stifled by conflicting politics and confusing norms.

This led me to invent The Simpel Kinetic Transformation Philosophy and the book you are reading today. Everything was built on my vision to use flexibility and organizational psychology to deliver something different... a meaningful transformation that can be measured in real and impactful ways. I had no plans to become as massive as the big guys, but I wanted to avoid being as soft and fuzzy as other corporate psychologists. I would thread the needle and help people along the way.

Huzzah! I had cracked the code. I had finally found who I was and what I wanted to be.

I guess that is what entrepreneurship is for me – finding myself or, as Sara puts it, just being me.

Over the years, I have learned that not everyone wants or needs to be an entrepreneur. However, like the sales skills mentioned above, I have also determined there are entrepreneurial skills everyone should have.

In this final section, I'll share what I've learned in my time as an entrepreneur and how you can use my experience in your business and life.

Entrepreneurship – the instinct to own my survival – proved vital in helping me uncover what makes me unique. (And you, as well.)

I thought my situation was hopeless.

I thought I would never find my place.

But because of the drive to survive I pushed myself to earn degree after degree while focusing on my family and building a happy life. Such self-actualization does not come without entrepreneurial skills.

As stated earlier, to lead you need a message that inspires and drives your goals. My message? Belief. What I wanted (and still want) more than anything is a feeling of being complete – with my self – with my family – and in my life. I believe I can get there and never stop trying. Once I realized this, everything changed.

After years of wondering, "Why am I not good enough," I finally stopped chasing everyone else's definition of success and pursued my own dreams. Combined with my unfailing determination to move forward and ability to fail up (plus a little luck), I created the right environment to find happiness.

Wherever you are in life (or in your company's lifecycle) cling to the value in everything you do – it's there.

Never be afraid to try. Never be afraid to learn. And never be afraid to be wrong.

Hey, with a little luck you may end up the next happiest M.B.A., psychologist with a background in law and a growing business. After all, everyone's path to success and self-actualization is different. Although my path was long, as Jared Jussim says in *Jerry McGuire*, "Hey... I don't have all the answers. In life, to be honest, I have failed as much as I have succeeded. But I love my life. I love my wife. And I wish you my kind of success."[74]

Key Takeaways:

- Entrepreneurial skills are important in both life and business.
- Being an entrepreneur means
    o Being yourself
    o Clinging to value
    o Never being afraid to try
    o Never being afraid to learn
    o Never being afraid to be wrong

CHAPTER 17: THE GOLDEN RULES

When I started Simpel and Associates, I never realized how alone I was in the professional world. After a twenty-year global career, I could count on my fingers the number of people I felt comfortable calling for advice, a lead, or anything else.

When you are in the corporate machine, you've got enough to worry about. The last thing you need is someone you met a while back on a project you barely remember taking up your valuable time and looking for favors. Perhaps I was wrong, but, as a new entrepreneur I always felt scared and uncomfortable to ask for help.

At first, I acted like I didn't care. "Screw it" – and I'd hit "Send." I tried not to be obtrusive. I never sent one email after another. Still, reaching out felt weird.

Then – it happened. For the first time in my life, a recipient *blocked me.* It was someone with whom I'd worked before and who had given me a sterling reference.

What the hell? Hard time for him? No use for me? Was I annoying?

Didn't matter. The sorry sucker didn't even have the decency to block my emails discreetly. I got a system generated message. Ouch!

I met wonderful people as well. Some, like my buddy, Ami, went above and beyond and provided the inspiration for pounding out my book. Others lent an ear when I got down about the unknown. A few were kind enough to help me edit some of my earlier works like *Agile at Transformations,* and to explore working and marketing together. Not all my initiatives were successful but there are some good, well-intentioned folks out there.

The experiences I had, especially in the early days of my business, shaped the true mission and principles by which my firm exists. Here they are in one place.

- Always add *real* value.
- Never rip off the customer.
- Treat everyone equally regardless of their level
- Never ghost anyone (unless they are becoming scary).
  - Remember, every engagement means someone is taking a risk on me.
- It's always personal.
  - Always have an answer even if it's "I don't know but will get back to you."
- Always use data to make/defend a position.

If any clients are reading my book, I hope I've always made good on my promises.

Adding real value is not secret code. I don't waste my clients' time with theoretical nonsense to nowhere. Whatever I do is outcome and result oriented. Short or long term, it's like a doctor giving medicine to a patient, everything I do relates directly to solving a question and nothing more.

Never ripping off the customer follows close behind. I am always scrupulous; I never overbill; I never pad expenses. More importantly, I ensure everything I do justifies my rate. If I am not adding value, I am the first to bring the fact to management's attention with options for how they can make the most of my diverse skill set. A laser focus on outcomes means clients often get far more impact out of me than from other, less multi-dimensional consultants. Because I look for opportunities to add consequential outcomes, my clients know I am a partner in value maximization and waste avoidance.

Treating everyone properly is much harder to pull off than it sounds. Being decent is only part of the equation. I strive to create an environment where interactions are meaningful and personable even during times of immense stress and change. As an organizational psychologist, I have built my career on always recognizing that everyone has value. My job is to help people recognize and maximize their own value and I enjoy this aspect of my job very much. When you view others in this way, you are not only doing the right thing but you are also creating an environment where everyone wants to win together.

Ghosting is a relatively new term for me. I heard it for the first time a few years ago. I had a contractor working for me and we were talking about personal stuff. He was telling me about his latest girlfriend.

"I really liked her," he said. "Then, she started ghosting me."

I was going to say "Huh", but I put two and two together and understood he meant she was ignoring him with extreme prejudice.

How friggin' rude. You go out with someone, even if only a few times, and then you act like you've been abducted by aliens? Unless this guy was a nut, and he certainly did not seem like it, he could have at least received a "thanks but no thanks" response.

To the best of my knowledge, I have never ghosted anyone. Even when someone frightened me, I lengthened my response time – but I never cut someone off without a word. Almost no one – and notice I said "almost" – deserves such treatment and I find the contemporary trend of ghosting about as mature as "the cool kids table" in every 1980s "teenage angst" movie. If everyone is useful, a basic premise in my life and business, then intentionally making them feel "less than" represents – at the very least – a substantial lack of common decency.

When a client signs an engagement, he/she is *taking a risk* – rolling the dice and buying into my rap (and rep). When a client decides to use my services, it is one of the best feelings in the world.

While the elation of winning a client is great, it is more

important to remember what the win represents: thousands of hours of work, prioritizing the client's needs over my own, and someone putting their ass on the line – for me.

The last of those is huge. At all times, I remember that someone went out on a limb and said, "We need to hire this guy." I want everything I do to make that person proud and to bring them recognition and reward.

Since we are talking about the person behind the signature, I would be remiss not to mention a truism I learned the hard way: No matter what anyone tells you, it's never just business – it is *always* personal. My father was the first person to teach me this idea and it has held true without fail. Many of us spend far more time at work than we do at home with our loved ones. In some ways, our work lives are more important (at least from an hourly investment standpoint) than our personal stuff. Most of us would have significantly different personal situations if we did not have work. We rely on "the paycheck" to provide all the things we have and enjoy – and we count on "bringing home the bacon" to provide for the people we love. When we mess up at work and make someone else look bad or, on the other side, we blow it out and make someone look good, we make an indelible and important impact on someone's life.

During my time with the big consulting firms, I experienced this message firsthand. I was leading a massive transformation and the partner on the account was getting concerned. The client was not relating to me as I needed or wanted. The partner came on site to give me advice and to help me out.

The partner was a gentleman's gentleman – brilliant – class act. He understood the numbers in a way you don't see every day. He'd been a partner in other Big 4 firms, sold a startup, and now leads a major private equity fund. When he spoke, I paid attention.

We caught up in the break room over the kind of coffee that trades convenience for any semblance of taste. He asked how I thought things were going. My reply told him my team and I were working 15-hour days, seven days a week, and we could not keep it up. The deal was way under sold and we needed to redesign the team structure.

He furrowed his brow at the idea of a loss of margin. We engaged in a detailed discussion about the work, the workload, and the quality of the team. No one on the team was sufficiently equipped and we were buckling under the stress.

I closed the conversation by saying I felt all the issues on our team were resulting in a loss of relationship with the client. I was worried it would not end well...especially for me. Realizing my trepidation, the partner's eyes softened, and he asked me what I had done to make my relationship with the client more personal.

I asked for some explanation. He explained the key nature of personal relationships – the basis of trust in all of business. His clients knew him personally, or felt like they did, and stayed loyal to him because of the connection.

Business relationships are different from what we have with those we love, but they are still very personal. They require attention and service and must be grounded in trust, honesty, and good will.

The last two points go together.

BS makes for a good story but not for a successful business deal. *Have the data and be ready with an answer.* My clients know if they ask me a direct question, they will always receive a direct answer. They may not like what they hear, but they will always know where I stand – and why. I always base my conclusions on data. If you hate my opinion, you will have a way to refute it. Handing in fact-based work represents a powerful way to generate honest, good discussion and unbiased decision making.

So, now you know the key principles by which I operate (and by extension, the way my firm works). Everything crystallizes into a neat package – be a good person, work hard, give, and earn respect.

Basic – traditional – maybe even a little boring. But they never fail, and I am proud to carry them with me into work every day.

Key Takeaways:

- Define who you are and what you stand for
- When you understand your why and stick to it, you will never be lost

CHAPTER 18: BECAUSE MY PARTNER IS LOST IN SOUTH AMERICA

It was a few years ago and I was in my mid-thirties. I was hanging out at home babysitting my kids and a buddy came by to say hello. As usual, we caught up about politics, life, children, and anything else that excites middle aged guys in the suburbs. We drifted onto the topic of a mutual friend who had been involved in some shady dealings. (He's straightened up, but it was close for a while.)

We marveled about how wild and cool this guy was and lamented our own mundane realities. Then my friend reminded me how a life of partying and freedom came with a major cost to health, quality of life, and – most important – family. My friend concluded our discussion with one of his great lines: "Sometimes not being the coolest person in the room is a good thing".

While we all want to be popular, successful, or recognized, the truth is, sometimes it's not so bad to be uncool. As Lester Bangs says in Almost Famous:

> Oh, man, you made friends with 'em. See, friend-ship is the booze they feed ya... 'cause they want ya to get drunk on feeling like you belong.... Because they make you feel cool, and hey, I met you. You are not cool.... Because we are uncool. You know, while

women will always be a problem for guys like us. Most of the great art in the world is about that very problem. Good-looking people—they got no spine; their art never lasts. And they get the girls, but we're smarter....'cause great art is about...guilt and long-ing, and, you know, love disguised as sex, and sex disguised as love, and hey, let's face it, you've got a big head start... I'm always home, I'm uncool.... You're doin' great. The only true currency in this bankrupt world is what you share with someone else when you're uncool. My advice to you, I know you think these guys are your friends, if you wanna be a true friend to 'em, be honest and unmerciful.[75]

As year one of Simpel and Associates moved into year two, I began to really think about my business model. Would I be an incubator? A consulting firm? An outsourcer?

One of the businesses I explored was the burgeoning can-nabis market. With the expansion of legalized marijuana, the sector was ripe for explosive growth. Even inhalation had been modernized. From volcanos to vaporizers to pens, it was a bon-anza of Cheech and Chong[76] proportions.

Recognizing the potential of this nascent, and now legal, industry, I was intrigued.

I started networking and quickly met some, ah, very interesting people one of whom was a grower out west looking to introduce a new product. We had a great conversation about his ambitions and the advantages we would enjoy in a partner-ship. He owned acres of premium land, had a license to grow re-creational marijuana, and had established a brand name ripe for expansion.

Jackpot!

With my business savvy advice, we could make loads. I jumped right in.

I prepared a Statement of Work (SoW) and an engagement letter. But every time I tried to schedule time with "Dude," he blew the meeting off for this or that reason.

With my frustration growing, I demanded a meeting with

my new client and his partner. Either they signed the SoW and we began, or I was done.

Days passed without a response to my ultimatum. I got pissed. The client had wasted my time and now, after months, he was ghosting. I called him.

The client answered. "Uh, yep."

"Hey, this is Nathan, what's going on?"

After a little banter, he said, "Sorry about being so flaky but I'm having to pick up a lot of slack because my partner is lost in South America."

We ended the call amicably. I thanked him for his time and told him to call me when he wanted to proceed with the SoW.

When I hung up, I felt good. For the first time in my entrepreneurial life, I had stood up for myself and left on good terms. I was in control and was making good decisions rather than desperate ones, a sign of growth.

Then I remembered what he'd said near the end of the conversation: "My partner is lost in South America."

Huh?

Was he saying his partner was missing or just off having fun?

I envisioned the FBI showing up at my door. I had only a two-degree of "Kevin Bacon separation"[77] from the guy in Brazil or Argentina or wherever.[78] I started worrying about my family, my wife, and my children. I realized I lacked the expertise or stomach for the *ganja* business and would be more than happy to watch from the sidelines.

Upon stepping back for a moment, I realized I'd lost my way. I am not indicting the marijuana industry, but it is not for me – and never was. My lust for achievement blinded me to the realities (and intricacies) of the business. In this instance, and everywhere else, I needed to stay in my own lane.

Ideas like entering the legal marijuana business illustrates the challenge many entrepreneurs face. In the hunt for revenue and to define ourselves, we sometimes look in places we don't belong. Sure, we need to test our limits – the definition of being an entrepreneur – but as Polonius says, "To thine own self be true."[79] Never allow yourself to get lost in an idea or the fluff surrounding it. If an idea in its most simple form does not work for you, no matter what you do, you will fail.

I want to mention a case from the T.V. show, *Shark Tank*.[80] First off, I love the show. While I know it is loosely scripted and heavily edited, it still provides the viewer with an opportunity to reflect on what the next big idea could look like. It also lets viewers compare their decision-making acumen with actual multi-millionaires.

For some reason, the presentation I remember most was for a product known as "Shuffles."

Picture yourself in your kitchen. You just spilled a cup of juice. What do you do? You can either: A) Get on your hands and knees and start scrubbing, or B) Drop some heavy cloth on the floor and move it around with your feet (shuffle – get it?). I don't know about you, but Option B strikes me as a hell of a lot more appealing.

I could imagine the entrepreneur in her kitchen when the lightbulb went off in her head. "Hey, everyone spills stuff. I wonder if there is a product?"

You know the story – it almost never changes from week to week. The woman had invested her life's savings on her idea and the sharks were her last hope to keep her dream alive. Unfortunately, none of them took the bait and she left – despondent. (The segment aired a few years ago. Since I couldn't find it with a Google search, I am guessing the idea is "deader than Elvis."[81])

When the segment closed, I was livid. Given all the dopey ideas the sharks had invested in, why not something as obvious as Shuffles? It had a cute name and a relatable CEO. Surely Laurie could've marketed it on QVC.

A few days later I was in my kitchen and dropped my kid's cup. Bam, there it was, a real-life opportunity to use Shuffles. I dropped a few paper towels on the floor and got to "Shufflin'."

After five seconds I realized a few things.

- The concept was, in truth, incredibly stupid.
  - Paper towels are inexpensive, and Shuffles would certainly cost more.
- Was I really going to wash a Shuffle after I finished?
- Shuffling in sticky stuff sucks.
  - I ultimately had to get on my knees and spray to eliminate the remaining "ick."

The sharks knew more than I did – the product would have been cost prohibitive and purposeless. How did I miss the problems? But the inventor had not seen the issues either and had burned every dollar she had.

Entrepreneurs sometimes get lost in products and passion. Had she spoken with anyone before investing her life's savings? What about a product developer from Proctor and Gamble? After a twenty-minute conversation, she could have gathered enough data to dissuade her from the fool's errand and yet, she stood at the feet of millionaires and begged for a shot.

As my dad likes to say, "Nothing wrong with failing as long as you fail up." By virtue of trying, the presenter on *Shark* Tank learned something of the nature of entrepreneurship. Maybe she figured out not to quit her day job. Either way, for an entrepreneur, it is all about the adventure and the means to the end. And while putting goals and structure around your concept helps to ensure you don't waste your time and end up Shuffling across South America, if the core idea stinks, sometimes you just face the facts, cut your losses, and try again.

In the early days of Simpel and Associates, I was leading a large global carve out. For the first time, my consulting career was gelling. My natural ability to build a relationship with a client was working to my advantage. I was making friends and building deep and meaningful contacts. I was also making mistakes but hey, you take the bad with the good.

During my first major engagement I met one of the most fascinating and brilliant people ever: Eric Christopher. A great leader, Eric had an outstanding resume filled with all the biggest name consulting firms and had enjoyed early and widespread success. He owned the room when he entered. His presence changed the atmosphere in business and social settings alike.

He was cool about it, too.

I admired his consistency. Every day for six months, we met daily for a 15-minute 1x1 where there was no bullshit. He came prepared with real questions and expected nothing less than excellence from me.

Day after day, I arrived at work with prepared "outcomes" as Eric called them. I would give my roll up and stand ready to go as deep as he wanted on any subject at any time. A very intense time and one of the best learning experiences of my life.

During our interactions, I worked to listen to every pearl of advice he shared. I made the most of every minute because I knew I was in the presence of brilliance.

Two days before our first big presentation together, I had stayed up all night working. I wanted the presentation to be perfect. I wordsmithed every slide and cultivated every diagram. As I stood back and looked at my masterpiece, I knew Eric would love it.

After a night of fitful anticipation, I presented to Eric. After five minutes, he stopped me and dropped this nugget:

"Consultants always make the same mistake of doing too much."

He was spot on. Consultants always feel they need to justify their high billing rates and "credentialize" their expertise. So, they craft elaborate presentations at the end of which – who the hell cares? Think about it. After someone loses a gazillion dollars, they never think back and say, "But that presentation was a monster!"

Eric wanted me to use the tried and true KISS method ("Keep It Simple, Stupid). If the idea is good, people will get it. Once they do, they will own it and implement it. Conversely if the idea stinks and no one buys it, at least people didn't waste a whole lot of time and money.

When an idea is simple, you can pivot at any time – make appropriate adjustments – and work together to make it a win. You've heard it before: "You have to break a few eggs to make an omelet."

The same is true during any engagement. I used to grind over the minutia. I worried about smoothing out every unhappy person – greasing the path for every resister. But when I stopped trying to do too much, I built results quicker, more people got on board, and everyone was – eventually happier. It helped when I determined resistance is not so much opposition as it is a reaction to fear. Nothing removes fear as much as a leader who keeps putting numbers up in the "W" column. Bottom line: everyone wants to be a part of a winning team.

So, the next time you are faced with an important task, meeting, or what have you, remember, things do not have to be complicated to be great.

If the steak is "solid," you don't need any sauce.

Key Takeaways:

• While it is always good to learn and experiment, this can sometimes take us to places we don't belong. Stick to your Golden Rules and you will never get too far astray

• Never allow yourself to get lost in an idea or the fluff surrounding it. If the core idea stinks, sometimes you just face the facts, cut your losses, and try again

• There is nothing wrong with failing as long as you fail up and grow from it

• The next time you are faced with an important task, meeting, or what have you, remember, things do not have to be complicated to be great

CHAPTER 19:
THE UNSEXY KEY
TO SUCCESS –
REPETITION

During the Great Recession, like many other people, I experienced one of the greatest challenges of my career. I had been working for a leading global bank when out of nowhere, the financial crisis hit, and I was laid off. Everyone in our department, including the boss, was let go to reduce headcount.

Because I was unhappy in work at the time, my attitude was not the greatest: *If it works out, great; if not, no worries because I'll get a nice package and a goodbye cake.* In this case, I bit off more than I could chew.

The crisis took on Old Testament proportions. The great banks I had admired for years were reduced to financial fairy dust and my entire team's life along with it.

Was the world ending? Would I ever find work?

After losing my job, depression landed on me like a satellite. Being the ever- aggressive salesperson, I tried using my nascent organization skills to organize a new consulting business. I called on everyone from my old boss to a lawyer I knew who had also been recently let go. I attempted to cobble something together but quickly realized I was building Frankenstein's monster.

Out of options and down on my luck, my wife came along

with a bright idea, as always. We had been invited to our neighbors' home for Friday night dinner and she felt it would be good for me to go. They were much older than we were, but how much worse could the evening be than *the total collapse of every global financial market?*

It was close.

Course after boring course came and went. The food had no taste – which matched the total lack of joy in my heart. Sara tried to cheer me up. I stared back through soulless, despondent eyes. I could not imagine how I would have the energy to stand up to go home. And then it happened.

Out of nowhere, one of the guests mentioned something about guitar.

In my boldest, young-man-who-knows-it-all cockiness, I offered my opinion. "Jimmy Page is the greatest guitarist of all time."

Our host, Adam, responded, "The greatest in which genre?"

Then, the geezer schooled me on everything there is to know about guitar. Apparently, in his younger years, he'd been what his wife called a "lost boy" and he turned to music for help.

I left the evening with a smile and a momentary peace. I knew the tranquility would only last until the Monday morning storm of depression, but – for the moment – my heart was full, and my spirit was restored.

Only the Monday morning downer never came. On Sunday, Adam (our host) stopped by. He was not a rich man by any stretch, but he was so happy to meet another music enthusiast that he had bought me my very first guitar.

Since that moment, I spent time studying four instruments: guitar, harmonica, violin, and voice. While our daughter is the real talent (the voice of an angel), I am content to share a song or two from time to time.

Adam's simple act of generosity sealed a friendship. He and I began to hang out. We would talk about music into the wee hours. He taught me a little about the guitar – never asked for or accepted a dime. We listened to all genres and analyzed composition and style.

Without this unique form of "friendship therapy," I doubt I would be writing this book. I am forever grateful to Adam – my neighbor and my friend.

Despite being the son of a famous rabbi and community leader, Adam had not pursued the rabbinate. Rather, he took what seemed to me to be a boring, 9–5 government job. Indeed, he was the black sheep of his family. Still, he was the happiest guy I'd ever met.

The more I got to know him, the more I appreciated his amazing life. Adam's wonderful wife loved him with the ferocity of a Bengal tiger. When they were together, their affection radiated with force field intensity.

They had three children, all of whom went to college, landed great jobs, and were happily married. Most of my other neighbors had lousy looking yards – these guys had meticulously maintained grounds – and a pool.

By his own admission, his work was not intellectually challenging. Sounded like hell on earth to me, but he loved it because it gave him the time to research and enjoy his true passion, music – specifically blues guitar. What's more, he even had a clear path to retirement by sixty-two.

I once asked Adam the secret to his success. His response was simple. "I never try to hit home runs. I look for singles and doubles."

Instead of flash and splash, my neighbor focused on the consistent delivery of the basics. He told me story after story about this or that wealthy acquaintance who hit it big, flew too close to the sun,[82] had an affair, and lost all their money. He grinned a little and said, "With a little time even I start looking pretty good."

And you know what? He was right.

We all want explosive growth right away but sometimes it's okay to hit singles and doubles. To get to explosive growth you sometimes need to start slowly and build a sensible plan.

This is a good thing and will save you lots of pain later.

I've already mentioned the value of a good core idea. Never compromise on quality in favor of *pizazz* because, believe me, it will not be worth it in the end. Given that 50% of startups fail within five years (with the most common reason being lack of capital and debt), I am sure there are a lot of folks who wished they had checked to make sure there was water in the pool before they decided to dive in.

Once you have the idea, cultivate it with clear and realistic expectations. It takes time and feels slow at first, but I have found if you stay at it, things will eventually work. Simple consistency represents a recipe for success in anything you do.

Case in point; I built Simpel and Associates' business plan on a basic concept I called the 1, 3, 5.[83]

- Year 1: Survival. We take whatever we can get to keep the lights on
- Year 3: Invest. Flesh out what works, achieve some sense of stability and grow
- Year 5: Hit cruising altitude

Year One was hard. When I experienced my first unhappy client and then my first dry spell, I almost fell apart. But I remembered the immortal advice of Jimmy Dugan: "It's supposed to be hard. If it wasn't hard, everyone would do it. The hard is what makes it great."[84]

I kept hoping and praying for the big break, which never comes as fast as you expect. But because I took whatever I could find during my first twelve months, I had enough funding to weather the storm and to see the dawning of Year Two.

At the time of this writing, I am in the middle of Year Four. I can finally make a real investment in the business without fear of imminent bankruptcy. I feel comfortable in my own skin and am starting to make more strategic decisions. I can turn down clients if I don't think we are a good fit. My ideas are taking shape and I am gaining a following. Sure, I still worry about money, but I am "feeling stronger every day."

My next checkpoint comes next year. Like everyone else,

I cannot guarantee it will all work out. But I can still easily trace my experience back to my core idea and the steps I took along the way. By staying consistent, having patience, and setting realistic aims, I am poised to blow the doors off if I choose. It feels less scary and I am more confident in success. That in of itself is priceless.

Best of all, because I am racking up wins along the way, it has never been boring. That says a lot from a person who lacked serious patience and consistency through the better part of his childhood.

So, the next time the mountain seems high and unattainable, remember, Derek Jeter was never a great homerun hitter, yet in my personal view he is the greatest New York Yankee ever.[85] By consistently putting the ball in play and sticking with a good team he won five World Series and retired as a first ballot Hall of Famer.

Who knows, the same may be true for you and your business.

Key Takeaways:

- Large scale change seldom occurs with a big bang. It often requires a slow and steady build. They key is to be consistent and flexible and to use momentum (Kinetic Energy) to see it through
- As stated previously, the most important thing is a clear idea. You don't need all the facts but the basic idea, a bias for action and practice

CHAPTER 20: I AM ME

We are approaching the final chapter of my life's work, so I want to start the process of ending our relationship for now. A cornerstone of my methodology is putting as much effort into the exit as I do into the entrance. After all, if a client spends a ton of money on me then watches his/her business collapse two days after I leave, what good have I done? No one likes indentured servitude, least of all me; the same should be true with this book. Hopefully, you enjoyed the read and want to come back for my next book or lecture. If not, thanks for your time.

Let's close with one of the most important keys to entrepreneurial success: self-awareness.

My self-awareness came after a significant time on a long and winding road. I now have a very good sense of my weaknesses and I am no longer self-conscious about them. Whether it is my non-stop, energetic approach to things or my natural, situational anxiety when things do not go my way, I am proud of who I am and everything that comes along with it.

It wasn't always true.

For a long time, I doubted myself. I made innumerable stupid mistakes that gave me more pain than I needed.

At least I eventually found the Rosetta Stone,[86] cracked my own code, and altered the course of my life.

Oh, don't get me wrong – I still struggle with the "know thyself" business. I can attribute my internal wrestling match to environment, experience, a lack of self-confidence, or a host of other reasons. While I had ambition (and managed a continual pattern of failing up), a dearth of vision and clarity early in my career prohibited me from listening to, accepting, and reacting to feedback.

To succeed in my own new venture, I realized I had to overcome my limitations. People want to be heard and an inability (or refusal) to ingest feedback would permanently prevent me from being the professional my clients needed, expected, and deserved.

I thought back to one of the pivotal projects in my career: the front, middle and back office outsourcing project I mentioned earlier. The manager from my firm was "Cecil."

The client, "Shaun," was brilliant and understood all too well what motivated consultants. Using this knowledge he tweaked us without mercy.

Even though my team was clearly working fifteen-hour days, seven days a week, Shaun always compared us to another consulting firm that was working for him on a separate venture. He pitted us against each other with comments like, "How come the other team is always here late and you guys leave early?" Bullshit. He knew the poking would bring out my sensitivities as the team lead and drive me harder.

One day, like all initiatives, the project hit a hiccup. Shaun sat us down and proceeded to cut through Cecil like Moses parting the Red Sea.

Cecil was no pushover. He was young and brilliant. He knew how to lead and how to operate at a senior level. He was a good consultant.

Over the course of a half hour, Shaun let him have it. Cecil did not say a word. He sat there, took it, and responded with simple answers like, "I hear you" and "Let me have a chance to think and come back to you on Monday with an answer." It was an amazing display of restraint because, despite the immense pressure, Cecil never broke, never lost his cool, and most importantly, never tried to lateral the blame to me.

After the dust settled, Cecil went back to work – and Shaun respected the hell out of him.

Cecil ultimately made partner because he understood the importance of feedback – even when it comes in a brutal, sometimes personal, form. Without it, we cannot adjust to meet our clients' needs.

Feedback has always been tough for me. I work hard – as hard as anyone – and I was always baffled when anyone thought my efforts were less than perfect. In retrospect, I realize a few things:

- Feedback is not always about me.
- If used properly, feedback can create collaboration.
- When you are unafraid to listen, you can learn a lot.

Sometimes feedback is really about the sender. Sometimes the client (or a loved one) is trying to tell you, "I am scared" without admitting it themselves. Self-actualization and awareness are about delivering feedback in a constructive fashion, something not everyone can do.

From time to time, people need to vent. Absorb the punches and process the real message. The faster you move past the words and decipher the message, the faster you will uncover the helpful part.

Once I unraveled the mystery of feedback, I learned to understand my father and our relationship changed from combative to supportive and interdependent – very powerful.

When you take the time to understand the person giving the feedback and the context in which you receive it, you can make almost any project more collaborative and effective.

The day I sat down to first write this chapter I received a call from a talent agent. She markets my services and handles my back-office work, which lets me focus on client service and delivery. Our relationship is critically important and one I manage with great care.

For the last several weeks, we have been working on a deal with a very cool company. (We'll call it BOCO for purposes of the story.) The proposal has been accepted and I have sent a signed copy of the SoW. Unfortunately, no one at BOCO has signed the agreement and it has not been returned (as is standard operating practice). Because of the delay, we have a significant issue because BOCO wants us to begin in less than a week (typical).

Of all the agents I have worked with, "Marge" is particularly good. She is honest, responsive, and transparent. She busts it on my behalf, and I am enriched by our association.

Anyway, we are nearing the end of day three and I am getting frustrate.

Marge: Hello

Nathan: Hi, Marge. Just letting you know I can no longer commit to the start date.

Marge: Nathan, what's the matter? BOCO wants you to start and now you won't agree?

Nathan: I only get paid when I work. Waiting on the promise of employment doesn't go very far with me.

Marge: I don't get it – you know they want you to do the job.

Nathan: Waiting on the promise of work is not an option. Without a signed contract I am taking too great a risk and I cannot afford it. It is also unfair on a personal level.

I asked my agent if she tended to anyone elderly. She said "No." I reminded her the project was located near one of my family members – someone I look after. To keep costs down, I had offered to stay with the family member rather than a hotel. The family member, elderly and alone, was excited to organize his plans around me and I am not in the habit of letting people down, especially those close to me.

Without a signed agreement, I could not commit, which meant I could not confirm with my family member – unfair on an emotional level and impolite to a cost-conscious individual going out of his way to accommodate me.

Once my agent understood the position the client was putting me in, she straightened everything out. The client signed and the engagement was a smashing success. My agent listened to me and took the time to understand my needs. I was open in communicating what I was feeling. So, we worked together for a great outcome. When used in this open and honest way, feedback becomes an opportunity to find ways to work together towards shared outcomes: the hallmark of any successful team.

You can also see the emergence of Maslow's famous postulation[87] at work. In the early stage of my business (aka Year One) I was at the lowest rung of the pyramid: survival. Had this situation happened to me a year or so ago, I would have given the start date and bitten my tongue about my elderly relative. I would have begun the project with a chip on my shoulder and probably self-sabotaged as a result.

Now that I have grown and become more accepting of feedback, not only do I find opportunities for improvement but I also see positive encouragement. For example, looking at this interaction I realize now that I am finally in a place where I am confident and self-assured enough to say what I really feel. Like many, finding self-esteem can be a very hard thing. Sometimes our lack of self-confidence prevents us from seeing the good in situations. We then endlessly seek positive reaffirmations via "atta boys." This is where many teams fail as people develop sharp elbows and look for reassurance over the good of the team. Knowing this is why the best managers encourage independent teams rather than trying to control ever move as we saw earlier in the book.

Unlike earlier in my career, I now know that:
- There will be other opportunities,
- I have great people behind me,
- I believe in myself and my capabilities,
- I am proud of how far I have come.
- I really am an artist and I am damn proud it.

With this understanding I can now navigate better and handle relationships differently. This enables me to act as my wife says from a "position of power" rather than always being afraid to speak up.

When used properly, feedback and self-awareness become critical tools for determining and acting on strategy. When you understand your limits, it is funny how much more you can do, which leads you to pursue – rather than avoid – feedback, however harsh or uncomfortable.

Well, there you have it. The no holds barred story of me, what I learned, and how I developed a philosophy for managing massive change and finding a sense of satisfaction in everything I do. It has been a crazy road and I hope the ride will not end any time soon.

I am sure I will continue to fail along the way – I may even embarrass myself again – but at least I will know I took my shot and that is more than most.

After all, an artist without rejection is just a dreamer.

Here's to happy transforming.

Key Takeaways:

- An ability to seek out and accept feedback is one of the most important determinants for success
- Remember:
    - o Feedback is not always about you
    - o Break feedback into data
    - o Build it into your plan
    - o Always be honest with yourself
    - o Approach feedback scientifically

Epilogue: The Path Forward

Phew! I can't believe I did it. I am so glad to have told my story and I hope the lessons and techniques provided will help you better yourself, your family, your team, or your company.

There is so much here, I am guessing you are probably a bit lost. Where to begin? How can I begin to incorporate what I have learned here into my own life?

To be honest, sometimes it just boils down to Yoda's famous line: "Do or do not – there is no try."[88]

Unpackaging this, for a long time, I found the Jedi Master's statement puzzling and silly. Seriously, if you don't "try," how can you do something? No one conquers anything the first time out.

Sometimes I buy a pack of cigarettes. Sometimes I say something hurtful to someone I love. After all, I'm as human as the next guy – and we all screw up.

When I fail, I get down, but after so many years of working on myself, instead of kicking myself or wallowing in my failure, I just pick myself up, dust myself off, and resume business as usual. For a long time, I couldn't. Any setback triggered self-destructive behavior.

What a waste of time.

My transformation began as a teenager. I looked at myself in a bathroom mirror at my friend John's house. I'd barely graduated high school. I'd read exactly *one* book in my life: *Private Parts* by Howard Stern.[89] I was going nowhere in every sense of the word. If I ever wanted to have more – to do better – to amount to anything – I needed to change.

Right then.

I was just a kid, but when I decided to change, I was all in. I left the bathroom, gathered my things, exited with barely a word, and never went back. I drove home and told my mother that I wanted to take the SAT.

I did terribly. But the very action of doing, of starting, put me on the right path.

It's the same with any change. Sometimes you have no money or time or feel so down you cannot imagine a time when things will be better. No matter how desperately you want to change, maybe you just can't put your finger on what is wrong or how to conquer it?

It is always better to start doing something than to keep doing nothing. Like my father said, sometimes you just need to stop worrying so much and start writing. By virtue of beginning, even if everything may not be exactly right, you take the most important step.

If you don't know where to begin, see if you can identify what I call "no regrets moves" and act on them.

No regrets moves are actions that you will never be upset about – no matter what. Simple things – like getting out of bed and walking around the block or being more conscious about saying thank you to another person. With a little consistency, you will be surprised how quickly the wins add up, lead to motivation (and ultimately to a real plan), and move you forward in a more transformational way. You don't always need a huge initiative to start transforming. You only need an open mind and a willingness to try.

One final story...

As mentioned previously, before I started college, I spent a year studying in Israel.

Like any highly religious seminar, there wasn't much to do – that was the point. We weren't there to have fun but to learn the Torah and to be inspired by the people and culture around us. I went to Israel primarily because I didn't have much else going on at the time and after my *ah ha* moment, the trip felt like the best way to shake things up. (Remember what I said about changing your surroundings?)

The days passed, and I tried to engage in deep religious study. For some reason, unlike all my friends and family members, it never stuck. Where others found intellectual growth, I found boredom. Where others saw the secrets of the Universe, I uncovered inconsistency. When you are young, there are very few things worse than feeling differently from everyone around you.

It was terrible for me. I ached to fit in – to be like everyone else. I wanted to find the peace and growth my friends had. I longed for the tranquility my parents and rabbis assured me I *would* find.

Still, I was – nowhere.

The thudding emptiness of my life hurt worse because *I cared.*

In the middle of the monotony and sadness, for some reason, I always made time to listen to the words of the late, great Rabbi P.

Every Thursday night, Rabbi P. gave a talk about the modern world, his views of what it meant, and what was important. He was quite focused on the ultra-observance side of things but for some reason, I felt I could relate to him.

He always concluded his hour-long talk with the exact same phrase:

"May we all be *zocheh* (worthy) to live life the way it should be lived"

To which the audience would reply *amen* (truth).

He delivered his "tag line" with such verve, I always felt I could get through another day or another week and continue my path of growth. I was doing my best to live the way I should – with truth and authenticity.

On the last Thursday of the year, Rabbi P. gave an exceptional speech. Everyone was riveted. Before he "signed off," Rabbi P. handed out little pieces of paper upon which were printed his famous phrase. He thanked us for listening to him and said he hoped we enjoyed his talks and would be worthy to live life the way it should be... with truth. Then, without hesitation, he said his line, we collectively said amen, and all went our separate ways.

I kept that little piece of paper in my wallet for more than 10 years. Every so often, I would pull it out and peruse it – do a little mental inventory – make sure I was following through.

Even after I lost the little scrap of paper, I routinely did the mental exercise to ensure I was on track.

Over twenty years later, at our first sabbath in a new community, we went to synagogue and I met someone who is now a good friend. We talked like newly introduced people do and eventually got around to "Jewish Geography." "Oh, you lived in Paramus. Do you know Henry Greenblatt?"

"Yes. So, you went to Rutgers? Did you ever meet Isaac Schwartz of the Long Island Schartzes?"

When I mentioned where I went to school in Israel, my friend's face changed.

"What's wrong?"

"Did you ever know Rabbi P.?"

"Loved the good Rabbi." And I launched into a long explanation of the sign-off phrase and the slip of paper and the introspection, and how I'd lost the paper.

My new acquaintance had grown up in a very small observant community in Maine and Rabbi P. had been his best childhood friend. He told me all sorts of great stories and I smiled and laughed throughout the entire conversation – until the end.

"How is the good Rabbi?" I asked.

My companion's face fell. "Rabbi P. died a few years ago – rare blood cancer. He was forty."

The reality of my own mortality cut through my heart.

I've seen so many go – and too many go too soon. Truth is, no one knows when their number is up. The risks and difficult changes we all experience can come at any time and it is not always easy to brush yourself off and keep on going. And yet, humanity continues, life continues, and I continue.

In my younger days, I was stuck in a serious rut. I was sad, depressed, and failing. Things deteriorated during the first half of my career when I could not find happiness or my footing. But I stayed at it and twenty-years later, I find myself with my beautiful wife, family, and new friends. Content.

Perseverance and hope are the bedrock human traits that keep us going when things look like they are at their worst.

They are the spirit of the song of humanity and I am glad that I took the hard road even though it began with more than a few faltering steps.

With that, I thank you again for reading my book and in the words of the late, great Rabbi P.:

"May we all be *zocheh* to live life the way it should be lived. Amen!"

---

[1] Avicii, ne. Tim Berling, suffered from various health and mental issues. He bled out (April 20, 2018) from apparent self-inflicted injuries from a broken wine bottle.

[2] For the record, Fosbury developed the technique when he was in high school. His wife and children came along much later.

[3] If you've never seen *The Usual Suspects*, pop some corn, grab a beverage, and settle in for 106 minutes of mind bending, cinematic storytelling.

[4] © 2019, Moshe Nathaniel Gampel

[5] Jesse Bruce Pinkman was played with manic intensity by Aaron Paul on Vince Gilligan's smash hit, *Breaking Bad.* The only character (besides Walter White) to appear in every episode, Jesse put three Emmy Awards for acting on Mr. Paul's mantel.

[6] "An object in motion stays in motion with the same speed and in the same direction unless acted upon by an unbalanced force." Sir Isaac Newton ("First Law of Motion")

[7] Union Navy Admiral David Farragut, Battle of Mobile Bay, August 5, 1864.

[8] Kurt Lewin (1890-1947) is considered as the father of social psychology

[9] The boundary defining the region of space around a black hole from which nothing (not even light) can escape.

[10] For a more detailed breakdown of how I interpret the cycles experienced during a transformational change, please see Agile for Transformations, the basis for Just in Time Staffing, 2017 all rights reserved.

[11] Note to self: Do not invite this guy to a bachelor party.

[12] Subtitled "What the Dying Had to Teach Doctors, Nurses, Clergy & Their Own Families. Available at: https://www.amazon.com/Death-Dying-Doctors-Nurses-Families/dp/1476775540

[13] Agile is a methodology or approach to work that began as a way for IT organizations to deliver products faster and with increased interaction with the end customer. For the Agile Manifesto, see: https://agilemanifesto.org/

[14] The idea of using the product as it is being built. This requires the team to be unafraid of feedback and mistakes so they can learn and adjust in real time

to the optimal solution.

[15] See The Simpel Transformation Framework, Copyright Simpel and Associates, 2019

[16] In the military, "challenge coins" designate membership in a special unit or participation in a specific tour of duty. Though of small intrinsic value, the coins are highly prized by those who earn them.

[17] Orthodox Jews attend services every day.

[18] Person who oversees a project plan and ensure all tasks towards a larger end goal are completed on time and on budget.

[19] Queen of Hearts in *Adventures in Wonderland* by Lewis Carroll

[20] Company that offered a technology to automate test grading.

[21] Boards of Education everywhere – take note!

[22] Note: My "study" is empirical, not scientific. So, grain of salt.

[23] Contrary to the urban myth, no one called 9-1-1 to report "the poor man having a seizure."

[24] No one knows who said it first, but in an article in *The Journal of Marriage and Family,* Professor Deborah Carr of Rutgers University defended the maxim's veracity.

[25] https://zumtobel.us/media/inspiration_-filters_sheets/2016-06-14_21-57-33/Zumtobel_Study_Whitepaper_Industry-and-Engineering_Productivity-through-Dynamic-Lighting.pdffing

[26] Of course, this is an oft-repeated line from the classic '80s movie *Ferris Buehler's Day Off.*

[27] Sadly, while I have been advocating for this for years; it took the pandemic of 2020 for companies to get it right - finally.

[28] Need to add reference. Simpel and Associates, 2019

[29] Played with great flair by Robin Wright and Carey Ewells in *The Princess Bride.* Buttercup: "We'll never survive." Westley: "Nonsense. You're only saying that because no one ever has."

[30] A distinction without a difference.

[31] This is a true story. My friend at the time responded that I was nuts. Years later, Sara and I bumped into him on the street. After about five minutes of reconnecting my friend said, "Wait a minute. Isn't this the girl you said you were going to marry?" It was a very good night.

[32] Michael Myers's villain from the *Austin Powers* series. "I didn't spend six years at Evil Medical College to be called 'Mister,' thank you very much."

[33] A term for the WWII generation, coined by Tom Brokaw.

[34] If this comes across as a little cold and binary please note, that this is

merely a reference to what will be a future work on a topic I call, "Just in Time Staffing" or (JiTS). This is an "idealist" concept whereby an organization can operate with peak efficiency because people are plug and play. The right person with the right skill is selected for the right job at the right time. This adds massive efficiency but also should benefit the employee because he/she is now focused on desired tasks at his/her own pace. The key is to establish and build this relationship from an equitable foundation.

[35] *The Ladykillers,* Coen Brothers. 2004. Starring Tom Hanks and Irma P. Hall

[36] William Makepeace Thackery, British, author, novelist, and illustrator best known for his satirical works

[37] Orion Pictures 1989 – "Strange things are afoot at the Circle K."

[38] *Bill and Ted's Excellent Adventure.* Oh – the characters say "dude" seventy times in the film. It is "most excellent."

[39] Though the last draft lottery call was December 7, 1972, American men are still required to register for the Selective Service within 30 days of their 18th birthdays.

[40] See for yourself: https://www.youtube.com/watch?v=DPq4kjCVeb4

[41] https://medium.com/@emilystroia/losing-your-job-can-feel-like-the-death-of-a-loved-one-79b3c7d60f62 https://www.livescience.com/8122-job-loss-takes-toll-mental-health.

[42] The lead character's name was William Wallace, but you knew who he was talking about. The 1995 movie, directed by and starring Mel Gibson, won the Best Picture Oscar.

[43] Played by Brendan Gleeson

[44] James Cosmo, a veteran with 233 acting credits, gave an outstanding performance

[45] A Kinetic Transformation term or outcome. Transformation, if done properly, represents an opportunity to achieve irrational returns.

[46] Remember scenario 1 and 2 from the last chapter?

[47] Lead musicians and singers Moshe Tanenbaum, and Yossi Berktin are Hasidic Orthodox Jews who play "Uncle Moishy" and lead the "Mitzvah Men" in song and verse that expresses the observant religious lifestyle of Orthodox Judaism. *Something Jewish, May 2, 2004*

[48] Formed in 1970 in London, the original lineup of Freddie Mercury, Brian May, Roger Taylor, and John Deacon continues to thrill rock and roll fans who listen to the group's classics. *Scaramouche, Scaramouche, can you do the fandango!*

[49] Electronic Dance Music

[50] See: The story of Sisyphus – the Father eternal frustration.

[51] Think this is easy? Check out Ed Sheeran's video for *Shape of You* and let me

know what you think

[52] ABC television, 2004-2010. Known for non-linear narratives.

[53] Spoiler alert! Read no further if you want to be surprised.

[54] Okay, I'm off the soapbox now.

[55] The original quotation belongs to James Carville, political strategist for Bill Clinton. In 1992, considering President Bush's unpopularity and a recession, Carville kept hammering the phrase, "It's the economy, stupid."

[56] A lamentable collection of great artists who died at age 27. Members include Jimi Hendrix, Janis Joplin, Jim Morrison, and Kurt Cobain.

[57] To be clear, yes, this is a veiled knock at the utter and irresponsible waste by leading consulting firms when producing beautiful presentations. Unless you are going to hang it on a wall, why would you ever spend hundreds of thousands of dollars of personnel hours to produce a presentation? They should be simple and to the point with a minimal amount spent on pretty pictures. Sorry, everyone has their own industry soap box; this is mine.

[58] For only $12, you can enjoy unlimited 30-minute rides around New York City. Visit www.citibikesnyc.com for more details.

[59] A small motorcycle with bicycle pedals. The term "moped" was coined in Sweden in 1952.

[60] An electric bike, pedal bike, car sharing system run by Neutron Holdings, Inc. in various cities around the world

[61] U.S. Department of Health and Human Services. *The Health Consequences of Smoking—50 Years of Progress: A Report of the Surgeon General. Atlanta: U.S. Department of Health and Human Services, Centers for Disease Control and Prevention*, National Center for Chronic Disease Prevention and Health Promotion, Office on Smoking and Health, 2014 [accessed 2019 Feb 1].

[62] Ibid.

[63] Creamer MR, Wang TW, Babb S, et al. *Tobacco Product Use and Cessation Indicators Among Adults – United States, 2018. Morbidity and Mortality Weekly Report 2019;* volume 68(issue 45): pages. [accessed 2019 Nov 25].

[64] https://www.opinionoutpost.com/en/blog/if-youre-stumped-on-who-wants-to-be-a-millionaire-always-ask-the-audience#.XmZsX6hKguU

[65] "Order of magnitude" = shop talk for "How much is all this stuff going to cost?"

[66] Robert Redford played Roy Hobbs in the 1984 film about a gifted but unlucky baseball player. (Didn't hurt that Kim Bassinger was in the movie.)

[67] Business as usual. These are the day to day tasks performed in a business operation

[68] Foreign Account Tax Compliance Act. In anticipation of this change to tax reporting, banks collectively spent billions. The act was delayed multiple

times and resulted in countless, needless changes to business lines.

[69] https://www.businessinsider.com/highly-successful-high-school-drop-outs-2016-6

[70] Far from some tepid, inspirational graduation trope, Lewis wrote the words to Mary William Shelburne, a woman who was dying. In an ironic twist, the great theologian and writer died five months later.

[71] 2009 American romantic comedy-drama film directed by Ken Kwapis and distributed by Warner Brothers.

[72] Born in Pittsburgh in 1874, the witty Ms. Stein is best known for two quotations: "A rose is a rose is a rose," and "There is no there there."

[73] James McKinsey (1889-1937) – professor of accounting at the University of Chicago and founder of McKinsey & Company, then chairman of the board of Marshall Field & Company.

[74] Played by Dicky Fox, *Jerry McGuire*, 1996. Not the most memorable line from the movie (anyone else tired of "Show me the money"?) – but certainly one worth remembering.

[75] Philip Seymour Hoffman as Lester Bangs in *Almost Famous*, 2000 – written by Cameron Crowe.

[76] Cheech Marin and Tommy Chong – legendary comedy team known particularly for their cinematic devotion to consumption of massive quantities of ganja. Their movies include *Still Smokin'*, *Up in Smoke*, and *Nice Dreams*. "Whoa, Quarter Pounder."

[77] The parlor game, *Six Degrees of Kevin Bacon*, postulates that any actor or actress can be connected to Kevin Bacon (over 90 career film and television credits) within no more than six moves (6°).

[78] Approximately $2/3^{rd}$ the size of North America, South America consists of 6.888 million square miles. That's a lot of area in which to "find Waldo."

[79] Polonius, *Hamlet*, Act 1, Scene 3.

[80] ABC Network reality show – debuted August 9, 2009.

[81] Elvis Aaron Presley died August 16, 1977. "The King."

[82] Icarus, the tragic figure of Greek mythology, ignored his father's instructions and soared too high in the sky on wings made of bird feathers and wax. When the boy "flew too close to the sun," the wax melted, the wings disintegrated, and the lad plunged to his death. Carelessness, ego, and a reckless attitude regularly lead to destruction.

[83] Ironically and by pure luck, I discovered that variants of this strategic model have been reflected in numerous articles on the topic of entrepreneurism. I guess I was on to something and didn't even know it.

[84] Tom Hanks as Jimmy Dugan in *A League of Their Own*, Columbia Pictures, 1992. He was talking about baseball, but the words apply to anything worth doing and doing well.

[85] To all you Babe Ruth, Mickey Mantle, or whatever fans, you can't argue with the Jeter led team's dominance and his role. If you can... well, tough. You already bought the book and made it this far ◆◆

[86] Discovered in 1799, the Rosetta Stone held the key to deciphering Egyptian hieroglyphics.

[87] The Hierarchy of Needs from *A Theory of Human Motivation,* Abraham Maslow, 1943. They are physiological, safety, love, esteem, and self-actualization.

[88] *The Empire Strikes Back,* 1980. Remember when we thought Yoda might be the weirdest character in the *Star Wars* saga? Jar Jar Binks anyone?

[89] Somehow the book was not nominated for the 1993 Nobel Prize in Literature.

Made in the USA
Middletown, DE
10 January 2022

57745222R00116